Interpreting Scripture

A Catholic Response to Fundamentalism

Edwin Daschbach, SVD

Religious Education Division
Wm. C. Brown Company Publishers
Dubuque, Iowa

Nihil Obstat:
   Rev. Eugene S. Ostrowski
   Censor Deputatus

Imprimi Potest:
   Rev. Raymond Lennon, SVD
   Provincial

Imprimatur:
   ✠Joseph H. Hodges, D.D.
   Bishop of Wheeling-Charleston

November 30, 1984

The Nihil Obstat and Imprimatur are official declarations that a
book or pamphlet is free of doctrinal or moral error. No
implication is contained therein that those who have granted
the Nihil Obstat or Imprimatur agree with the contents,
opinions or statements expressed.

All Scripture quotations from the *New American Bible*

This book is dedicated to the Catholic Church
and to my parents
who, because of their devout and deeply committed
Catholic lives, have inspired me to a similar
fulfilling commitment.

Contents

Foreword

In the pages that follow I have tried to present a way of interpreting God's Word that is faithful to the directives of the Catholic Church. Those directives recognize the methods contemporary biblical scholars use to arrive at the meanings intended by both authors of Scripture: the human and the divine.

Hesitant readers can rest assured that the opinions and interpretations offered are not radical. They are representative of responsible centrist biblical scholarship.

There are probably very few Catholics today who have not been, in one way or the other, influenced by the upsurge in biblical fundamentalism. This book was written for that large group of Catholics who have not really accepted fundamentalism's approaches, but who desire some updating in response to that challenge.

My intent is to help these Catholics approach Scripture in an enlightened way that does justice to discoveries and insights of solid biblical scholarship. But just as importantly, I will try to show how that scholarship can aid Catholics in bringing Scripture to the important place it should occupy in their lives.

I have limited this book to a length that would be inviting. Nothing so scares a potential reader as a formidable tome! But this attempt at brevity can also have its own type of disappointments. Much could be treated only in the most scanty fashion.

I believe, however, that there is a real value in presenting such a concise overview of Scripture scholarship. It may succeed in opening readers' minds to the rich insights scholarly research has to offer for the pages of Scripture. It can then have the pleasant result of inspiring these readers to become enthusiastic about further research on their own into questions that have frequently plagued them in their Bible reading.

I owe special gratitude to Bishop Joseph H. Hodges, bishop of the Wheeling-Charleston diocese of West Virginia, for giving his attention to this manuscript despite his serious illness. I shouldn't be surprised. Such concerned dedication has been the consistent trademark of everything this much-loved bishop has done for his people. I also appreciate the review of Father Eugene

Ostrowski. With the various hats he wears in the diocesan office, he really didn't need the added burden my manuscript provided. He nevertheless undertook the assignment with charity and care. My provincial, Father Raymond Lennon, SVD, and his predecessors afforded me the opportunity to write this book by assigning me to work in West Virginia. I'm grateful for the eleven year experience and for their constant support and encouragement. A special note of thanks to Sister Terisse Zosso, S.Sp.S., Ph.D., Associate Professor of Theology at Divine Word College, Epworth, Iowa. Her detailed comments and suggestions reminded me once again that there will probably never be an end to this author's need to improve his manuscripts!

Wm. C. Brown editorial staff members Sandra Hirstein and Marilyn Bowers Gorun support that contention by the editorial alterations they brought to these pages. Their professional skills resulted in a "fine-tuned" manuscript. May God bless all of these individuals because of their selfless dedication.

Chapter One

The Need for Biblical Scholarship

What role does Scripture scholarship play in helping us truly grow as God's people? How does our study of the insights scholars bring to us help us better understand God's Word? How can an improved knowledge of Scripture aid us in giving it a more central role in our spiritual lives, make it speak better to us today? Why not, as fundamentalists direct, just read the Bible ourselves and forget about all this biblical criticism business?

These are important questions, and I hope my manner of presentation does justice to the kind of response needed. At the outset several observations are needed to stress the "whys" behind the need for "everyday Catholics" to be acquainted with the results of modern biblical scholarship.

1. We can only love what we know. While simple, uneducated people may feel comfortable with the limited knowledge gained from what they read in the Bible alone, the knowledge required for the great mass of properly schooled Americans must be comparable to other levels of learning. A boyhood friend of mine with only a grade school understanding of Catholicism later became a nuclear physicist. His adherence to the Catholic Church didn't last very long. How could it, when his religious education didn't keep pace with his secular knowledge?

The same thing can happen to our estimation of Scripture. Unless we learn to appreciate it with the mentality of an educated person, the Bible's value is equally threatened. Our respect for Scripture won't be very great if we continue to experience countless problems in its pages and take no serious steps to solve them.

2. If Catholics are not at least partially versed in the proper interpretation of Scripture as shown by responsible biblical scholarship, they become part of the reader problem that effectively exposes the Bible to ridicule. Christians should always be part of the solution, not part of the problem. The contradictions, disagreements between passages, and conflicts with science are abundant (as will be indicated throughout this book). The critical spirit of our twentieth century culture shows little patience with religious practitioners whose beliefs take no account of truly valid discoveries in the fields of archaeology, linguistics, and other related sciences that have a bearing on the pages of Scripture. Our responsibility to reach out to an unbelieving world mandates that the message we present is at least respectable.

3. An Indian priest friend studying in this country once told me how amazed he was at the gullibility of so many Americans. He was referring to the uncritical manner in which we attach ourselves to, and dote upon, religious charlatans from India who are literally laughed out of that country.

These and other cult leaders who roam our land would not find so many easy prey if our youth, in particular, were better instructed in the things of God. True, the cults would still tend to attract them by their false lure of community and belonging, but the safety catch of a solid foundation in Catholic belief and the true meaning of Scripture would prove a too awesome bulwark for those cults to handle. Cults would be seen for their superficial and ultimately empty appeal. There is a wisdom gracing those educated in religion and Scripture, a certain sophistication, if you will, a depth of perspective into the workings of God that causes cult attractions to appear naive.

4. The results of scriptural scholarship help us understand and value more lovingly our own humanity. We see the great importance the human element played in the transmission and recording of God's Word. God respected humankind's deficiencies and freedom in the process, evident from the limitations found in the texts. Besides the contradictions and inconsistencies, there are historical mistakes, scientific mistakes, even religious errors. And yet it remains our firm conviction that God's guidance was present through it all. There must be something tremendously valuable about our human qualities that caused God to respect them so

much that He did not force a change, that caused Him indeed to become one of us and one with us. Appreciating our humanity will help us live more lovingly together.

5. Scholarship helps us learn to better appreciate the genuine and full humanity of Jesus as well. We see Jesus' lack of a detailed knowledge about the future. He is shown to make errors when quoting Scripture. He shared the same mistaken notions as other people of his time about many things. These and similar insights about Jesus from scholars lead us to understand better the depths of the love of God for us—that he truly lowered Himself to share our existence, to identify with our sufferings, our limitations. This makes Him much more appealing than a god who would have only "faked" human existence limitations. It's hard to relate to a divinity who is not genuine.

6. The results of scholarship help us understand ever more forcefully the critical part the Church plays in bringing Jesus Christ to us. Catholics, in particular, because of the importance they place on Tradition, will find this supportive. Many of their peers have recently reveled in questioning that connection. "Why do I need the Church if I have my Bible?" is a variance frequently found in rural America.

When scholars share with us their discovery that a belief in Jesus as "God" was not reflected in Church writings until the latter quarter of the first century, roughly A.D. 70–100, and we counter with the claim: "But John's Gospel shows Thomas clearly calling Jesus *God* in a resurrection appearance," we have zeroed in on the Church's major role in the formation of the Gospels. Scholars explain the apparent conflict by showing us how the Church's beliefs about Jesus, which the promised Spirit led them to understand, have been retrojected back into the Gospel fabric.

In the case of the confession of Thomas in John 20:28 referred to above, the Church and author of John put on Thomas's lips two words used for the one God Yahweh in the Old Testament: "My Lord and my God!" It is the clearest expression in the entire New Testament of Jesus being called "God" (Theos) and reflects how the Church had gradually come to a belief not clearly present in the lifetime of Jesus or in the years immediately after. Although our first reaction may be to view such an alteration as irresponsible tampering, to the Gospel authors and the Church it was a manner of fully expressing for posterity who Jesus really was.

There are innumerable other instances of such retrojection. We are led to see how the Gospels are not literal historical biographies of Jesus. They are theologies, catechisms of Church belief about him. Understanding this shows how useless it is to try to separate the Church from Christ. We may go our merry way believing that the Church is an unnecessary crutch that can easily be ignored. But Jesus' words will always be there to haunt us: "He who hears you, hears me."

The same Church that formed and preserved for us down through the centuries what we know of Jesus remains today a similar guide in understanding him. He always comes to us through his Church. We court disaster if we try to create a separation.

7. Of course, it's the message of the biblical teaching itself that becomes clearer because of scholarship. We'll find meanings to words that cannot be captured in a translation, themes that unite isolated episodes and discourses that can easily be lost. Scholars help us understand better, through an exposition of the author's themes, the context in which isolated passages occur. This is important, as can be shown from the classic example of the individual who, in seeking guidance for his life, opened his Bible to different locations and came upon: "He went out and hanged himself.". . . "Go and do likewise!" A failure to grasp properly an author's message can result in scriptural quoting to support our basest prejudices.

8. There can be no doubt about our Church's position regarding the importance of Scripture reading for the spiritual life of Catholics. Vatican II's document on Revelation states:

> *This sacred Synod correctly and specifically urges all the Christian faithful to learn by frequent reading of the divine Scriptures the "excelling knowledge of Jesus Christ" (Philippians 3:8). "For ignorance of the Scriptures is ignorance of Christ." Therefore, they should gladly put themselves in touch with the sacred text itself, whether it be through the liturgy, rich in the divine word, or through devotional reading, or through instructions suitable for the purpose and other aids which, in our time, are commendably available everywhere . . . And*

let them remember that prayer should accompany the reading of sacred Scripture, so that God and man may talk together; for "we speak to him when we pray; we hear him when we read the divine sayings."[1]

Since it is our Church's will, and unquestionably God's as well, that we develop lives nourished by the divine Word, the importance of any competent guidance that we can enlist cannot be stressed too strongly. Scripture scholars bring an expertise to the Bible that often results from a lifetime of dedication. We should value their contributions no less than we value the advice and direction of medical specialists in preserving our good physical health.

The great body of Scripture scholars are responsible men and women. They may lead us to places and views that we may initially want to avoid, but God, who authors all truth, cannot be absent from valid discoveries of that truth. Knowledge can only bring us to Him—and Him to us.

1. Walter Abbott and Joseph Gallagher, eds., "Revelation," *The Documents of Vatican II* (New York: America Press, 1966), section 25, page 127.

Chapter Two

Our Journey to Where We Are

I am a forty-six-year-old product of a predominantly Catholic education. During the earlier half of my twenty-four years of formal schooling, I was exposed to what could best be termed a fundamentally literalistic interpretation of Sacred Scripture. The Bible wasn't stressed much in the pre–Vatican II era, so I was spared any real crushing conflicts that might have resulted if I had given careful attention to biblical passages. I missed the discrepancies, the contradictions, the unscientific parts.

It never dawned on me to challenge the early chapters of Genesis by wondering how vegetation could be in existence before the sun was created to give it life, or where the woman came from who married Adam and Eve's son Cain. I never questioned whether the story of Adam and Eve itself was symbolic, or whether a snake actually spoke and tempted them. Darwinian evolution was "out there" somewhere, not of any real serious relevance to the Bible. I envisioned unskeptically a total worldwide flood covering everything, and Noah taking two of absolutely every living creature on board his ark. I pictured the prophet Jonah really clinging to a whale's interior.

And even if I would have had some doubts about any of these stories in the Old Testament, I would never have thought that anything could be amiss in the New Testament! The questioning about the accuracy of the story of Herod slaughtering the Innocents (Josephus, the Jewish writer who hated him and detailed all his crimes, is strangely silent about this one), the disagreement between the Synoptics (Matthew, Mark, and Luke) and John about the length of Jesus' public ministry (one year or three?), the difficulty in knowing what Jesus actually **did** say, since his words are so differently reported in the various Gospels—these problems were totally outside my experience. I probably would have been shocked to even hear of them. What the Bible said was literally true. It wasn't that we spent time defending that literalness; we just presumed it to be so.

But gradually, almost imperceptibly, things changed. I began to read material that cautiously questioned former presuppositions. Genesis in particular was increasingly subjected to a detailed analysis, and with that examination came questions about the scientific accuracy: whether Adam and Eve were only representations of the first human beings, whether indeed we had to hold to monogenism (one set of first parents) or could accept polygenism (multiple first parents simultaneously). What about original sin? Was it really, then, a sin that we "inherit" today?

In the aftermath of Vatican II, Scripture was brought into center stage for Catholics, and with that new position of importance more and more was written—and read. People were requesting Scripture courses and joining adult discussion groups with scriptural themes. We had come a long way in a relatively short time.

What caused the change in the importance now given to Scripture? How did Catholics progress from an educational system that supported a literalistic interpretation of God's Word to the situation today that instead strongly supports what is known as a "contextualist" approach?

Before the Twentieth Century

It might as well be stated clearly right at the beginning. The Catholic approach to interpreting God's Word, prior to our current renaissance in Bible scholarship, had some similarities to what we now criticize in fundamentalism.

Much scholarly work had been going on for two centuries following Father Richard Simon's (+1712) contributions that inaugurated modern biblical criticism. But the work was for the most part outside the auspices of the Catholic Church. It seems that the tension between traditional beliefs and the rationalism of the new approaches to Scripture caused extreme uneasiness in the Church. Catholic scholars took the danger-free and easy road of failing to distinguish between the philosophy behind the new critical methods and the methods and conclusions themselves, and therefore spent their time on safe and nonessential questions. It was all part of the siege mentality that afflicted the Church since the Protestant Reformation.

It must be admitted, however, that in many ways the new critical methods and insights raised more questions than could be properly answered. Scholars did not yet have sufficient tools to understand all the perplexing problems that arose in Scripture study. Furthermore, coupled with the Protestant doctrine of "Scripture alone" was the belief of the reformers that any two people in good faith, reading the same text, would come to the same true understanding. This principle was vitiated within a very short time when it was found that Luther and Zwingli could not even agree on the interpretation of Jesus' words: "This is my Body." Misuse of the Bible thus became widespread. No honored place was given in Protestantism to the critical role of Tradition in understanding the things of God. Catholics believed that the danger of biblical misuse justified a fear of personal interpretation of Scripture, something fundamentalists blame us for today.

We can understand, therefore, the hesitancy Catholics of the past exhibited in reading Scripture. In response to Protestantism's stress on the Bible, Catholics countered with a stress on Tradition.

Catholics should be fully aware, however, of their Church's directives today. With Vatican II, the importance of reading and praying God's Word has been emphasized as paramount for the flowering of a deep faith life. Since the Church has defined very few scriptural texts, Catholics should approach Bible reading with enthusiasm, not reserve. It is Catholic, as well as Protestant, belief that God truly speaks through the Bible's pages.

The Twentieth Century

Scripture scholar Father Raymond Brown divides our century into thirds regarding the Church's approach to Bible studies. The first period (1900–1940) was characterized by the Church's negative reaction to Modernism: a strong rejection of modern biblical criticism. The second period (1940–1970) witnessed the results of, in particular, Pope Pius XII's encyclical *Divino Afflante Spiritu:* a positive approach to modern biblical criticism and the Church's reluctant acceptance of it. The third period (1970–2000) involves "the painful assimilation of the implications of biblical criticism for Catholic doctrine, theology, and practice."[1]

The First Period: 1900–1940

These first forty years of the 1900s were particularly bleak ones for Catholic biblical learning. Pope Leo XIII in 1902 set up the Pontifical Biblical Commission (PBC) that expended efforts in spelling out guidelines pertaining to issues of concern to scholars. Its rulings were not infallible but, as Pius X pointed out, were "useful for the proper progress and the guidance of biblical scholarship along safe paths." The Commission's decisions were largely conservative, however, and had the immediate result of stymieing Catholic scholarship.[2]

At the same time that these Commission statements were being issued, two documents came from Rome attacking the dangers of Modernism. Both occurred in the summer of 1907. The first, a decree entitled *Lamentabili,* condemned sixty-five Modernist propositions. The second was the encyclical *Pascendi.*

Modernism

Modernism is the term given to the Catholic movement in the early 1900s that sought to adapt Catholicism to liberal Protestant writings of the late 1800s. Many of the problems of Modernism lay in its stress on the natural, instead of supernatural, way of coming to know God. It seemed almost to deny the supernatural character of revelation. Mixed with this unacceptable aspect were many positive points that indeed were later canonized by official Catholic Church approval. But Modernism's skepticism about the supernatural called into question how God is behind Scripture, and that rightly incensed Church authorities. Their response was outright, instead of selective, condemnation.

The lack of any deep concern for Scripture shown in my Catholic education even through the 1950s was probably a direct offshoot of these cautionary developments at the beginning of the twentieth century.

---

1. Raymond E. Brown, S.S., *The Virginal Conception and Bodily Resurrection of Jesus* (Ramsey, NJ: Paulist Press, 1973), 3.
2. In relation to the book of Genesis, to be treated later, it stated that the first three chapters had to be viewed as literally true history.

The Second Period: 1940–1970

But something happened in 1943 that changed everything. Pope Pius XII published an encyclical entitled *Divino Afflante Spiritu* that opened the door to modern scriptural studies. A great freedom was given to scholars to translate Scripture from the original Hebrew and Greek (instead of the Latin Vulgate) and to make generous use of literary forms (i.e., to recognize different types of literature in the Bible). Respectability was rightly accorded to the conclusions of science, and scholars were urged to see how a degree of accord could be arrived at with valid scientific discoveries. The Pope mentioned that Church authority had ruled on the meaning of very few Scripture texts, and therefore scholars had freedom to apply their tools widely.

Literal Sense of Scripture

The Pontiff further stated that the exegete's (scholar's) principal concern should be with Scripture's literal sense. By literal he meant the most basic sense, the meaning intended by the human authors.

It is true that in our attempts to understand any book of the Bible, we cannot be satisfied with simply discovering the intent of the writers. That helps us know what the writing **meant**, but not fully what it **can mean**. Many people who have no formal biblical education can still find a wealth of meaning for their lives from their daily Scripture reading. Furthermore, as Scripture scholar Raymond Brown tells us: ". . . the way in which the Church in its life, liturgy, and theology comes to understand the Bible is constitutive of 'biblical meaning' because it is chiefly in such a context that this collection is serving as the Bible for believers."[3]

However, basic to any broader meanings of the Bible is an understanding first of all of the authors' meaning when they wrote, the "literal" sense of the individual books. Father Brown thinks this "literal" sense should be extended to include any contributions that influenced the book's final form. It must not be confused with the position taken by many fundamentalists today who

3. Raymond E. Brown, S. S., *The Critical Meaning of the Bible* (Ramsey, NJ: Paulist Press, 1981), 34. See also Brown's comments in *The Churches the Apostles Left Behind* (Ramsey, NJ: Paulist Press, 1984): ". . . normally church tradition has not interpreted what a biblical author **meant**; it has interpreted what his work means to a living community. I am painfully aware that Catholics and Protestants can be at one as to what Scripture meant but divided as to what it means." (page 10)

seek to find in Scripture a kind of truth the original authors never intended, i.e., pronouncements on history and science.

It is unfortunate that the word "literal" is used in such a confusing way. A contextualist uses it to refer to both text and context (historical, cultural, and literary background) of given authors in establishing those authors' meanings. This was obviously what the Pope meant by "literal" because of the encouragement he gave to the use of, for example, literary forms. We call fundamentalists "literalists" or "literalistic interpreters" because they zero in on only the text in their efforts to understand Scripture. They effectively ignore the authors' meaning behind the text. The difference in approach is responsible for the conflict between Christian evolutionists and creation-science advocates.

The Bible is a religious book, a statement of theologies, a catechism of Jewish and then Christian beliefs, not a strict eyewitness account of historical events. Biblical scholarship attempts to uncover those beliefs. They comprise the "literal" meaning of texts, whatever the main writers and others contributed to the individual book's final form before its inclusion into the broader canon of Scripture. Since there was more than one writer of even individual books of Scripture and the meaning of any given book depends on not only the originating author but all subsequent authors in the writing process, the literal sense of Scripture must include them all.

Revocation of PBC's Decrees

In 1955, a decade after *Divino Afflante Spiritu,* the secretary of the Pontifical Biblical Commission officially revoked the early decisions of the Commission referred to above. Father Brown, in a footnote to his book, *The Virginal Conception and Bodily Resurrection of Jesus,* calls the attention of traditionalists to this revocation and reminds them: ". . . it is lucidly clear (and not a matter of theological opinion) that the secretary's statement frees Catholics from any obligation of adherence to those early Biblical Commission decrees in questions of authorship, date, historicity, etc."[4]

Furthermore, the personnel of the Commission was changed by Paul VI in 1971 to include, in place of cardinals, some of the most illustrious Catholic biblical scholars in the world.

4. Brown, *Virginal Conception,* 4.

Another boon for Scripture scholars was the 1964 Instruction of this Commission on the historicity of the Gospels. Among other things, it admitted that the Gospels do not include exactly or completely the words and deeds of Jesus. They are in different form than when first uttered or performed. This has wide ramifications for the study of how beliefs of the early Church conditioned the words and actions recorded in Scripture.

The Commission tells us that if we are to understand the Gospels, we must realize that the teachings and life of Jesus have gone through three stages in the process of being incorporated into the Scriptures we have today:

1. When Jesus taught his followers, he used the language and concepts they could easily understand.

2. The apostles clearly recognized his divinity after his resurrection.[5] With that insight they were able to better explain who Jesus really was. They used the various literary forms current to their time in transmitting that message.

3. Finally, the evangelists wrote their Gospels incorporating both the preached message and other writings about Jesus that had come down to them. They "selected some things, reduced others to a synthesis," and, in the process, altered the order in which events happened. Although the words of Jesus are somewhat changed, this in no way destroys the sense of what he preached.

Vatican II

The 1965 dogmatic constitution of Vatican II entitled *De Revelatione* strongly supported the freedom given to scholars by *Divino Afflante Spiritu*.

In an 1893 encyclical, *Providentissimus Deus,* Leo XIII had provided a very good understanding of inspiration, that process by which God is Scripture's author. He stated: "By supernatural power God so moved and impelled the human authors to write— He so assisted them when writing—that the things that He ordered and those only they first rightly understood, then willed

---

5. How soon afterwards still remains a problem because of an earlier mentioned point, namely, that it is only in the latter third of the first century that we find belief in the divinity of Jesus clearly reflected in Scripture.

faithfully to write down, and finally expressed in apt words and with infallible truth."

Vatican II's document added to that description by saying: ". . . the books of Scripture must be acknowledged as teaching firmly, faithfully, and without error that truth which God wanted put into the sacred writings for the sake of our salvation."[6]

In order that we may truly understand such truths, the Council stressed again the importance of literary forms: two simple words that make all the difference in the world between the Catholic Church's former way of reading Scripture and its way of approaching Scripture today, between a fundamentalist's manner of interpreting Scripture and the methods used by most other Christians. It is those two words that lie at the heart of the controversy between creation-science advocates who want to bring the Bible into public school classrooms and the supporters of evolution who view those efforts as misplaced.

The next chapter will take a close look at some of those forms to see how they enlighten our understanding of Scripture.

A Catholic Contextualist and Inspiration

The acceptance of literary forms in Scripture supposes a different way of reading the text. The Catholic Church, together with most mainline Christian Churches and therefore most Bible readers, now adopts a contextualist approach to God's Word. It admits divine authorship but recognizes as well a truly human authorship. The vast differences the various books exhibit in style, vocabulary, and growth in religious insights necessitate this. Language studies, historical and archaeological discoveries, for example, are brought to bear on the written word and help us to understand the context of the writing.

In reference to the opening chapters of Genesis, for example, ancient pagan religious writings contemporary with the biblical writings, or certainly known at that time, sometimes show remarkable similarities that cannot simply be excused as coincidences. In some cases, it can be shown that these pagan myths and folklore were used by Bible authors. In other cases, both the Bible story and myth seem to witness to a common ancient mythical tradition.

6. Abbott, *Documents Vatican II,* "Revelation," section 11, page 119.

14

All of this raises the question of how God can be viewed as the Bible's author. His authorship is certainly concerned with re ligious insights, for the Bible is essentially a religious book. God did not play the part of an historian or scientist. *Inspiration* is the usual term employed to describe His influence, but there is much disagreement on the concrete process involved. A stenographic interpretation is clearly ruled out. And any interpretation must somehow take into account the fact that in the study of any particular religious insight, the Bible's message cannot be understood unless the entire Bible is considered, not merely isolated books or passages. Later books do not merely enlighten, but truly correct earlier misleading statements.

The Bible seems to include "time-conditioned" religious beliefs, that is, Israelite religious beliefs that we know today are erroneous. The belief that comes easiest to mind is the ban the Israelites reportedly practiced in the Old Testament when conquering their enemies. An example is found in Deuteronomy 7:2 and Joshua 6:17–21, where a total massacre of men, women, and children is presented as the will of God. This primitive idea of God's will is absolutely false, even though it was a religious belief of the Israelites then.[7] There are similar examples in the New Testament, such as the expectation in 1 Thessalonians of an early parousia (return) of Jesus. Likewise, we can include the inadequate idea of Jesus as less than God which is found in the more primitive beliefs of the early Church and reflected in some texts of the New Testament. And I wonder if we could also include the unfavorable way Mark's Gospel views Jesus' mother Mary, only to be later "corrected" by Matthew and Luke.

In point of fact, as scholar Raymond Brown points out: "A good case can be made that any major book of the Bible taken by itself and pressed to its logical conclusion will lead to heretical distortions."[8]

Something of the pedagogy of God with His people is reflected here. Accepting and respecting the limitations of humankind, He only gradually acquaints them with various elements of

7. The conquest of the promised land was not as the book of Joshua presents it. The fierce battles seem, for the most part, to be attempts at grandiose folklore. It is quite likely that some skirmishes occurred. But savage destruction as reflected in the ban? Probably not. We are still rightly disturbed, however, that the Israelites even believed such barbarism to be God's will.

8. Brown, *Critical Meaning,* 32.

truth, instead of flooding them with an intensive illumination of all revelation at once. This would be something they couldn't bear, and it would furthermore go against the gradual process of learning that is a constant factor in everyone's life. God deeply respects our limitations and only enlightens us when we are ready to receive that enlightenment. The history of each of our own lives, upon reflection, should show that to us clearly.

Individual biblical books are to be seen, therefore, in relation to all the books together. The Bible "teaches without error that truth which God put into the Scripture for the sake of our salvation." But we can never understand that truth by simply looking at individual passages or even individual books. If we want to see the Bible as a channel by which the truth of God's revelation comes to us, then we must look at it as a whole.

Review and Discussion

1. Was your background, or the background of someone you know, similar to the unscientific Scripture background of Father Daschbach?

2. Is it easy to change our way of viewing Scripture? Why do many people resist that change?

3. What is the literal sense of Scripture?

4. How can Scripture **mean** something more than it **meant**?

5. Discuss the three stages through which the teaching and life of Jesus have gone in the process of being brought into the Bible.

6. What are time-conditioned religious beliefs?

7. In what sense is the entire Bible inspired?

8. In what sense is the Bible without error?

Chapter Three

Literary Forms

We simply cannot understand what the Bible's human authors intended unless we know the literary forms they used, the type of literature they utilized to frame their messages. One of the reasons this is a difficult undertaking is because the biblical authors never spell out for us what the forms were. The problem is further compounded by the combining of the seventy-three books together under one "The Bible" cover. It's not easy to escape the conclusion that they are all the same. Fundamentalists make that mistaken judgment. We should not.

Modern Scripture scholars, because of their discoveries of literature in existence outside the Bible in Old Testament times, have been able to better understand the wide variety of literature present in the Bible itself. These include different types of history, some more factual than others; poetry (also of different types); drama; legend; folklore; myth; parable; allegory; and others, including types we don't fully understand. The Bible is now seen as a remarkable collection of literature as rich and varied as we find available anywhere in the world today.

Can you imagine what a person's sense of twentieth century history would be if, a thousand years from now, he should pick up an historical novel written in 1980 about the same 1980s and not recognize its historical-novel literary form? We make the same mistake now by not acknowledging the difference between fact and fancy in biblical writings.

Literary Purposes

Our search for the author's intended meaning in his work is not ended when we discover the literary form, the type of literature he made use of in conveying his thoughts. A further important question concerns the author's **purpose** in using that literary form. Why did he make use of a parable? Why did he frame his thoughts in a myth or in folklore?

For example, in the Genesis account of Jacob's all-night wrestling match with God (Genesis 32:23–33), scholars notice how closely the story parallels a quite common theme in ancient folklore: divinities struggling with humans. In those mythical tales we often find exactly what occurred in the Jacob story: the encounter takes place at night by a stream, and the divine beings are forced to reveal something to their opponents. When we combine these similarities with the mysterious nature of the tale and see how the story gave a popular etymology to the place's name, *Penuel,* meaning "face of God,"[1] we realize that the biblical author was simply making use of the literary form of **folklore**.

The next question is: Why did he do so? Our answer is found in the fact that the angel changed Jacob's name to *Israel,* a word that includes in its meaning the idea of "struggling." The people sprung from Jacob are called *Israelites,* and any careful reader of the Old Testament won't miss how a "struggle with God" characterized their subsequent history. And yet they knew that they were a special people of God. The author reflected those characteristics by incorporating them in a story of one of their ancestors who "struggles" in a wrestling match with an "other-worldly being." The Jacob wrestling episode is a retrojection of later distinguishing elements of the Israelites back into an originating sire of that nation. Briefly, the story is probably totally fictitious but serves well to show the faith the Israelites espoused in a providential God watching over their voyage through history.

Is the story inspired by God? Of course! God guided the author's use of the mythical elements so that they could be tools to teach the lesson.

1. A similar example can be found in Genesis 19:12–26. Erosion over the years had carved bizarre shapes out of salt rocks along the Dead Sea's shores. The biblical author created, or used from folklore, a fanciful legend about Lot's wife being turned into a pillar of salt to give one of many popular, but fully imaginative, explanations for the phenomenon.

And let's not forget the "sciatic muscle" of verse 33. The wounding of Jacob would help remind the Israelites of their belief that no one can see God and live.

Parable

One very popular literary form is the parable. Found in secular literature and in both Old and New Testaments, it is a fictitious narrative meant (in the Bible) to convey a moral or spiritual lesson. One reading a parable should not become too concerned about the minor details. Authors use those merely to stir interest and to build dramatic tension. Concentration should be on the main point instead; that is what the author, under God's guiding inspiration, understood.

There could hardly be found a more beautiful example in any literature than Jesus' parable of the Prodigal Son (Luke 15:1–3, 11–32). It conveys God the Father's steadfast and outreaching love for the sinner and the special welcome waiting for him when he repents.

Being a missionary, I have a special affinity for the parable of the sower in Matthew 13:4–23. Speaking of the process of evangelization, Jesus shows how the response to hearing God's Word can run from harsh resistance to enthusiastic reception. We often find ourselves between those extremes. Some seek an emotional high in religion and are not prepared for stages of aridity or the patience needed for long-term ordinary living ("Part of it fell on rocky ground where it had little soil"). Others, for fear of the cross, become proficient compromisers of the gospel demands—prefer the pleasures of life, selecting only those aspects of Christianity that fit their comfortable style of living ("Again, part of the seed fell among thorns which grew up and choked it"). The ultimate frustration in all such individuals is that, somewhere along the way, they became innoculated with such a mild dose of Christianity that they were thenceforth immune to the real thing.

These allegorical applications, however, should not distract us from the point Jesus was essentially making: the superabundant blessings awaiting those who do enthusiastically accept and faithfully follow God's Word in life.

Jesus used many other parables to teach his people. They were filled with everyday and yet never-to-be-forgotten images. Although some fundamentalists tend to regard parables as having actually occurred (e.g., there really was a Prodigal Son, there really was a king who invited guests to his son's wedding and murdered those who didn't respond—cf. Matthew 22:1–7), we know from their literary form that they are fictitious, but nonetheless important pedagogical lessons.

Bible History

When the biblical author took the traditions of his people and wrote about their trip from Egypt and settling in the Promised Land, he used the literary form of the *historical novel.* This means we shouldn't expect total historical accuracy in what he tells us, especially in Exodus chapters one through fourteen in which we read of Moses' infancy, the plagues, and the crossing of the sea in flight from "all the chariots of Egypt." In both secular and biblical literature, historical novels are stories with a core of historical truth, or stories written against the backdrop of true historical events. In the above examples from Exodus, the author's point is to call attention once again to God's watchful care of the Israelite people and the need, therefore, of continued faith and trust in Him.

Biblical historical novels are characterized by *midrash.* This is the term scholars give to ". . . an edifying meditation on an earlier biblical utterance, an imaginative reconstruction of an episode, or the construction of a fictitious episode on the principles deduced from biblical materials."[2]

Many examples can be found in both Old and New Testaments. Matthew frequently makes use of it. In his stories of the astrologers bringing their gifts of gold, frankincense, and myrrh to the newborn Christ child, the flight into Egypt, and the slaughter of the Innocents (chapter 2), Matthew seems to make use of Old Testament passages for free composition. The references are given in his text (Micah 5:1, Hosea 11:1, and Jeremiah 31:15). Such quotations are not meant to imply that they are predicting the events listed. They are only springboards for Matthew's literary talents. At our location in history, it is nigh impossible to categorically rule on the historicity of these three scenes. All we can do is reflect on what Matthew meant by them, for this was his purpose in presenting us with the colorful tales.

2. John L. McKenzie, *Dictionary of the Bible* (New York: Macmillan Publishing Co., 1965), 575.

In moving through the Old Testament, the contextualist reader has no problem accepting the core history of the period of Judges. But the reader also knows that nations tend to idealize, to exaggerate their past. Colorful material is added as traditions are passed on by word of mouth. And because the contextualist doesn't get bogged down with details, the author's intent, the true meaning of Scripture, can be seen more clearly. It is again the loving providential care God extends to this people that is being prepared to give birth to His only Son. And the reader is reminded that as God cared for them, He also cares for me.

When dealing with the time of King David, as reported in the second book of Samuel, the contextualist is aware that a more accurate account is being given, for scholars say it was written soon after the events took place—some of the most objective ancient history.

Continuing the biblical journey, the reader encounters other works that look and sound like history, but are not.[3] Jonah, Tobit, Judith, Esther, and Daniel are really examples of midrash. The authors have created fictitious narratives from some points of Jewish law or belief.

Jonah fled just about "as far as he could go" (Tarshish) in trying to escape the call to preach God's love for the enemies of the Jewish people. But God would have none of it. The book is a protest against all forms of bigotry, particularly against the narrowness and hate Judaism manifested for its enemy persecutors after the exile.

The story of **Tobit**, which includes his son's ordeals in company with the angel Raphael, served to remind Jews that their prayers during times of suffering would be heard. Tobit is the pious Jew, ever-concerned for faithful adherence to prescriptions of the

---

3. We should always be conscious of how the point of the narrative has a lesson for us as well as for the original Israelite audience. Scripture is always a mirror held before our faces in which we see an image of ourselves. We also act as those people did. We too need the divine and human authors' message.

law. Like him, other Jews should also be patient under trial with the knowledge that the good they do will not go unrewarded.

Judith brings out clearly one of the literary techniques used by authors to subtly depict the fictitious nature of such works: deliberately change history! The king of Assyria is listed as Nebuchadnezzar, who in reality was king of Babylon. No Jew above the age of reason would have missed the intended misapplication. Furthermore, as McKenzie informs us, Judith was "an unlikely name for a Jewish woman." The theme is once more God's care and protection.

Esther details a heroine's success in saving the Jewish people in Persia from extinction. Important characteristics of the story indicate its improbability: permission for the Jews, having been rescued themselves, to slaughter their enemies; the absence of a place in history for Vashti as a wife of Xerxes. Tradition uses the tale as the basis for the Jewish feast of Purim. But in all likelihood the feast's real origin was somewhere else in antiquity, and Esther was composed as a substitute. The literary purpose is again God's providential care.

The bloodthirstiness of Esther, the barbarism of Judith and other Jewish heroes and heroines of antiquity bother our sensitivities today. Decapitations, the driving of spikes through heads, and the cutting off of foreskins revolt us. Unfortunately, however, that's the way it was, or at least how people thought. We don't crucify murderers anymore as the Romans did. We don't cut off hands of thieves, nor brand adulterers. Are we, however, any more civilized, we who drop atomic bombs on defenseless citizens of Japanese cities and join another superpower in threatening humankind's total obliteration? We may be more sophisticated, but it can be argued whether we're really any better.

Daniel is the first Old Testament example of apocalyptic literature. Later in our commentary on the book of Revelation we will discuss this strange literature in some detail. Daniel is also, as the works previously described, nonhistorical. It is a freely composed story dating to about 167 B.C. The author's intent is to encourage his fellow Jews who were undergoing the persecution of Antiochus Epiphanes. We can call it, therefore, "persecution" literature.

The beautiful story of Susanna's rescue from the accusations of two elders who had been bent on sinning with her is part of this book. It occurs as a lectionary reading in long and alternate short form on the Monday of the fifth week of Lent. For a culture such as ours, obsessed with sex and prone to promiscuity, the book's message of suffering that results and vindication-reward for those who resist is so important it should be included in a Sunday reading to benefit larger audiences.

Poetry

In our reading of the Old Testament book of Joshua, we suddenly come upon a rather astounding event. In the midst of a battle between the Israelites and Amorites,

Joshua prayed to the Lord, and said in the presence of Israel: Stand still, O sun at Gibeon, O moon, in the valley of Aijalon! And the sun stood still, and the moon stayed, While the nation took vengeance on its foes. (10:12–14)

Our fundamentalist brothers and sisters, in their literalistic interpretation of Scripture, believe this was an actual occurrence being narrated. The earth truly ceased to rotate! They argue that we shouldn't be surprised because the power of God has no limitations.

While agreeing with their view of God's limitless might, contextualists try to remind fundamentalists that the quotation is poetry. It is a symbolic expression of what was already narrated in verses 7–10. In that more realistic account, there is no reference to the sun's or moon's alteration. The literary form of poetry is noted for its extravagant and fanciful descriptions. Examples abound throughout the Bible.

Deuteronomy 32:13–14 says that God gave the Israelites

. . . honey to suck from its (the land's) rocks . . . with the cream of its finest wheat, and the foaming blood of its grapes. . . .

In Psalm 55:22 we read:

Softer than butter is his speech
   but war is in his heart;
His words are smoother than oil,
   but they are drawn swords.

25

In commemorating the Jordan's crossing, Psalm 114:3–6 sings:

The sea beheld and fled;
Jordan turned back.
The mountains skipped like rams,
the hills like the lambs of the flock.

And Isaiah 11:1 proclaims:

But a shoot shall sprout
from the stump of Jesse,
And from his roots a bud shall blossom.

In all such cases we know instantly that symbolism is being used.[4] Scripture scholar Joseph DeVault, S.J., wrote more than two decades ago:

Attempts have been made even in modern times to explain the sun's "standing still" on the basis of a prolonged daylight due to refraction of light, or as a meteor shower or some other such phenomenon. These pseudo-scientific "explanations" collapse of their own tortured weight. Happily, they are being replaced by a sane exegesis which recognizes the passage for what it is—a highly poetic version of an emotionally charged cry of Josue, who hoped for time, for daylight, in which to crush the enemy utterly. The enemy was crushed, so the time was granted, and this is expressed poetically in verse 13a, prosaically in verse 13b.[5]

Besides reminding us of the obvious use of poetic imagery in the above example from Joshua, scholars take pains to teach that "miracles should not be multiplied." This doesn't mean they deny the miraculous. In the life of Jesus, for example, the primitive tradition attesting that he was a worker of marvels is too strong to explain away all he did. This is important to remember, because there **are** works of Jesus described as miracles or exorcisms by the Gospel writers that present problems.

---

4. A later compiler of material in the book of Joshua adds his own reflections in verses 13b–14. He makes the same mistake as fundamentalists today, interpreting the poem as having recorded a true miraculous event.
5. Joseph De Vault, S.J., *The Book of Josue* (Ramsey, NJ: Paulist Press, 1960), 20.

For example, Mark 5:1–20 tells of a possessed man from Gerasene territory whom Jesus cured by sending the evil spirits into a large herd of swine. Among other difficulties with the story, better ancient manuscripts locate the incident in places six to thirty miles distant from any sea! Scholars feel this story is derived from early folklore about Jesus very similar to apocryphal material otherwise normally excluded from the canon of Scripture. It seems to be built around an exorcism Jesus performed but has been embellished in continuous retellings. The story's lesson for us in this visit to gentile territory is that we are to carry the gospel to peoples other than those of our own group or comfortable acquaintance.

In their position that "miracles should not be multiplied," scholars are calling our attention to the ways early nonscientific peoples viewed strange occurrences. What they didn't understand, they considered works of wonder. Changes in seasons, storms, and prolonged dry spells were attributed to the powers of the gods.

Furthermore, there were frequent attempts by biblical authors to use colorful and descriptive imagery to better bring out for readers meanings of events and persons not readily observable. This was clearly acknowledged by the 1964 Instruction of the Pontifical Biblical Commission which stated that in the deeds of Jesus we have today only "the form compiled and edited by the evangelists," not the deeds as they appeared in the original or first stage of tradition. The same warning can be applied to Old Testament materials. In other words, Bible authors in both Testaments often created stories to serve as theological reflections on the meaning of persons or happenings.

Behind scholarly reserve about miracles is humankind's dominion over creation attested to in Genesis. Although we believe strongly in a God who providentially watches over His creation, who cares a great deal how we live, He is still a God who deeply respects the laws He placed in nature and the gift of freedom given us. History has made it clear that God does not always step in to save humans from the stupidities into which sinful disobedience leads them, or to change nature to fit human beings' plans, hopes, and expectations. Although we can never deny to God the exercise of His powers when and where He wishes, we should be cautious in seeing miracles or expecting them everywhere. In the

Incarnation, God came to us through and in humanity; so He expects to work His ways today. His gift of salvation comes to us through our love and service of one another. He expects us to use our talents to solve our problems. "God helps those who help themselves" is more than a flippant saying. It bespeaks something terribly important about how God respects and works with what He has created.

Myth

Scholars often use the term *myth*. Our first reaction upon hearing this word is to immediately equate it with "false," "make-believe." Myth is therefore envisioned negatively.

But biblical scholars give a positive meaning to the word. For them, *myth* means simply that people, reflecting on something in the human condition, expressed their insights in story form. The stories have a deeply symbolic meaning. They are attempts to explain what normally lies beyond observation, to some extent outside human experiences.

Myth is therefore an attempt to express truth by the use of symbols. The symbols may or may not be historically true. In 1971 Father Andrew Greely published a book entitled *The Jesus Myth*. He wasn't attempting to deny that Jesus existed. Rather, he was using the term to point out the tremendous meanings present for us in this God-man, the marvelous insights into God's love for us that words cannot adequately express. Not simply giving messages dropped from clouds, but literally becoming one of us by taking on our frail humanity bespeaks a depth and extent of love and caring for His creatures that forever exhausts our feeble attempts to comprehend.

Often, however, myths are also fictitious events that authors use to convey important insights. Stories of creation in different religions are therefore myths, since no one was around to observe what happened. So are Adam and Eve, Cain and Abel, Noah's ark, etc. They never really existed exactly as described by the biblical authors. But **that** there were first parents who did wrong and whose descendants also went astray, **that** sin brings suffering to mankind: these are true experiences of history past as of history today. Myths are thus ways of expressing realities that occur or endure now in our midst.

Reading that there are myths present in the opening chapters of Genesis, therefore, shouldn't disturb us. The biblical authors were not concerned about relating accurate history or science. But they **were** concerned about teaching us the evil of sin and what happens when we close ourselves to God's loving care and direction.

There are other types of literary forms in the Bible, several of which—wisdom and apocalyptic—will be alluded to in a particular way in the following pages. In modern Bibles, short introductions that precede the various books acquaint readers with the specific form involved. If we take the time to read those prefacing remarks, we won't expect to find history where it's absent or confuse fact with symbol.

Review and Discussion

1. List some reasons why all the Bible books cannot be understood in the same way.

2. What do we mean by literary forms?

3. Someone has said that there are two basic kinds of history: History and history. Explain.

4. What do scholars mean when they say that "miracles should not be multiplied?"

5. Was it dishonest for Bible authors to make up stories?

6. What do scholars mean by myth? Is it the same as make-believe?

Chapter Four

Of Morals and Maxims

Three leadership classes could be recognized in Israel: priests, prophets, and wise men. The latter two, prophets and wise men, now occupy our attention.

Prophets and Prophecy

A major part of the Old Testament consists of either stories about prophets or prophetic writings. It is very easy for us today to misunderstand the notion of *prophecy.* In the everyday-Catholic's mind, prophecy triggers the definition "future prediction." But this is misleading. Prophets indeed were graced by God with keen perceptions of life and of the political movements of their day. But they weren't normally given a crystal-ball view of detailed future happenings. "However, insofar as the prophet offers an interpretation of events and discusses the consequences of one form of action or another, or of a failure to act, the prophet is indeed concerned with the future."[1]

Later when we discuss such things as "fuller" and "typological" senses of Scripture, we'll have a chance to see the nuanced way in which we must look at future "fulfillments" of what prophets said and wrote.

Prophets were not, then, crystal-ball gazers. They were "spokespersons for God." In particular, they stressed to people of their time the necessity of right living in relation to God and others.

1. Richard P. McBrien, *Catholicism* (Minneapolis: Winston Press, 1981), 230.

31

They emphasized rigorous adherence to monotheism, the worship of the one and only God Yahweh. Surrounded as the Israelites were by polytheists (believers in many gods) who, for example, comprised nine tenths of the land's population at the time of David, there was an ever-present need for that prophetic witness. And while the prophets preached punishment for transgressions, they were also the heralds of subsequent deliverance, especially in their Messianic teachings. A remnant would always survive to serve as a nucleus for a brilliant future.

Their teaching technique was not limited to words; at times they resorted to symbolic action. In the book of Isaiah, 20:2-3, the prophet was instructed by God to walk barefoot and nearly naked through the streets of Jerusalem for three years. In thus assuming the humiliating posture of a prisoner of war, he was showing the Israelites in a symbolic way the folly of joining Egypt and others in defiance of the powerful giant Assyria.

The prophets seem to have been primarily **mystics** similar to ones known in the Christian era: John, Paul, Augustine, Bernard, Julian of Norwich, John of the Cross, Teresa of Avila, etc. Many of us have some taste of their experience in our deeper moments of prayer. We suddenly see things in a way we never did before. God's ways seem to make so much sense, to be all that really matters. We consequently view events of our lives and of the world around us in a new penetrating light. We understand so much better the awesome importance of eternity over present passing time.

The mystical experiences of prophets were much more profound. These special encounters with God illumined the prophets so that they had visions of reality missed by others of their times. When they shared their insights, therefore, they usually met opposition.

The prophets were fiercely loyal to the God they served. Some of them went to even immoral lengths to preserve the peoples' fidelity to Him, including the encouragement they gave to conspiracy and murder. McKenzie shows how the prophet Elisha, in his opposition to the Israelite monarchy, encouraged Hazael, whom he knew believed in total war with the Israelites, to assassinate Aram's king Benhadad who had made a peace pact with Israel (2 Kings 8:7-15).[2]

2. McKenzie, *Dictionary,* 695.

We recall the sometimes hilarious story of Elijah's challenge to and taunting of the 450 false prophets of Baal on Mt. Carmel in 1 Kings 18:1–40. At the end of the holocaust that proved a success for Yahweh belief, Elijah directs:

"Seize the prophets of Baal. Let none of them escape!"
They were seized, and Elijah had them brought down to
the brook Kishon and there he slit their throats.

Of course the question can always be asked: How much of these stories is really accurate reporting? On the presumption that sufficient accuracy is present, we may make some observations.

Dispensationalism is the term given to a view of Bible history that denies the continuity of the Old and New Testaments and stresses instead the differences. According to this manner of thought, one might be able to conceive of a god (note the small "g") who condoned violent acts in the Old Testament such as the prophets sometimes favored. Dispensationalism has few followers, however, because it seems to reflect, among other things, a capricious god who is not really trustworthy. Scholars and the great majority of Christians conceive of a God who is love, both in Old Testament times as well as today. Violence and other unloving acts attributed to His initiation or approval are simply mistaken interpretations by biblical personages and authors. God was the same loving being in Old Testament times as He is today.

What we're saying, in other words, is that despite the genuine contacts these prophet-mystics had with God, they still were subject to misinterpretations. St. John of the Cross, a doctor of the Church whom trappist-author Thomas Merton once called "the greatest of all mystical theologians," recognized this difficulty, for even in the case of genuine saints, much illusion and error had been found. He counseled therefore that people who think they're receiving special directions from God in any sort of private revelation should ignore them. There's a terrible danger of self-delusion. Thinking they are doing God's will, they may instead be merely doing their own!

Apparently, the prophets, in initiating and supporting violence, **thought** God wanted them to do that. Their thinking was strongly influenced by the often violent and barbarous times in which they lived. But in His loving providence, God could have helped His people through their problems, through the apparent pitfalls present, without the "assistance" of such well-meaning, but morally wrong, behavior.

Having said this, however, we must acknowledge that prophets were otherwise great men of God. Their deficiencies only point out how God does not destroy the limitations of His creatures when He calls on their assistance.

Throughout subsequent history, this tendency of our divinity has been both a consolation and a discouragement. From its earliest years the prophetic nature of the Church of His Son has manifested traits that have caused observers to respond in one moment with praise and in another with derision. Its all too obvious human elements have both attracted and repelled. It will probably always be so. But we must still work to eliminate whatever we can in our Church and in our individual lives that make it hard for the world to find God in us. The split in Christianity, in particular, calls all Churches to recognize how frail even the best of us are. It calls us to acknowledge our common failures and to strive incessantly for unity so that the force of our prophetic Church voice, our speaking for God in twentieth century living, will not be diluted because of a failure to speak with one voice.

Wisdom Literature

*It is better to dwell in a corner of the housetop
than in a roomy house with a quarrelsome woman.
(Proverbs 21:9)*

*When one greets his neighbor with a bold voice in the
early morning,
a curse can be laid to his charge. (Proverbs 27:14)*

The category of "wisdom" writings covers Proverbs, Job, Ecclesiastes, Sirach (Ecclesiasticus), Song of Songs, Wisdom, and some psalms. The Israelite scribes who authored these books spent their time and creative abilities amassing, composing, and disseminating knowledge and maxims very similar to those of other ancient cultures from which they liberally borrowed. They taught how it "pays to be good," how to live successfully and be happy. Initially tied in with the guidance of Israel's monarchs, they later dispersed themselves throughout the land so that they might share their learning and insights with all the people.

Wisdom, as it appears in Scripture, is not always the same thing as morality, for morality cannot simply be identified with success and happiness. It is often more like the advantageous actions of the steward of the Gospels who took pains to cancel debts owed to his master so that the debtors would be receptive to the steward after that same master fired him. It is a wisdom that is "wise as a serpent," and "cunning as a fox." Actions performed may be quite immoral. Scholar McKenzie gives as an example the "wisdom" (cleverness, craftiness, shrewdness, depending upon the translation) exhibited by Jonadab in the advice he gave Absalom on how to rape Tamar, his sister (2 Samuel 13). Wisdom was thus a very broad and complex word.

Much of Israelite wisdom literature differed from secular wisdom, however, by the way scribes "colored" their material with belief in the one God, Yahweh. One was wise and lived successfully if he obeyed the law, feared Yahweh, and modeled his behavior on traditional insights. While teaching how to live successfully, however, wisdom literature often failed to confront problems. It taught how to live with them, but not really how to solve them.

Job

Job brings all of this to the fore by dealing with the question of suffering. Old answers didn't fit. Why do the good so often suffer? Such questioning opened minds to the eventual revelation of reward and punishment in another life, but that solution is not found in Job. He instead learns not to challenge the Lord who alone has the answers: "I have dealt with great things that I do not understand; things too wonderful for me, which I cannot know." (Job 42:3)

Scripture scholarship has pointed out that a belief in immortality is found only in later Old Testament works. Remembering this, we can better understand the concentration in earlier wisdom literature on being a success in this life, for death ended everything. There was, of course, Sheol, the abode of the dead beneath the earth. But no knowledge of reward or retribution was envisioned there; you couldn't be a "success" in Sheol.

Ecclesiastes

Like Job, **Ecclesiastes** takes a negative view on conventional wisdom. The theme resounds from the opening verses: "Vanity of vanity . . . all things are vanity! What profit has man from all the labor which he toils at under the sun?" The book is especially remembered for its "appointed times" of chapter 3: times to be born and die, to kill and heal, to weep and laugh, to tear down and to build, etc.

Strangely, in the "anti" or "critical" wisdom that fills its pages, of all wisdom literature, Ecclesiastes probably comes closest in singing the praises of true wisdom. And here we see its justification for being included among the inspired books of Scripture. In their efforts to categorize and expound how wisdom could be practiced, the scribes had only managed to substitute human ingenuity for divine omnipotence. If man had all the answers, what use was there for God?

Ecclesiastes, like Job, sounds the death knoll for such attempts at independence. By confronting the deficiencies in wisdom literature, they offered the purification of wise reflection on the "otherness" of God who will not, who cannot, be categorized or stereotyped.

Its lesson is an important reminder for us today that our material possessions, our scientific knowledge, our beauty, our talents offer no real security in the quest for meaning in life. Suicides of Marilyn Monroes, of famous individuals who seem to have so much going for them "in the world's eyes," are twentieth century living parables of the message from Ecclesiastes. All efforts at success are ultimately futile. Our hearts are made for God and will not be secure in the possession or knowledge of anything less.

Wisdom

In the limitations of earlier wisdom books, we see once again the lesson of divine patience. God allowed religiously inadequate works in Scripture as stepping stones to further and fuller revelations. As with wisdom literature, so in other books of the Bible, we find religious concepts and beliefs woefully incomplete without the revelation that comes from other later books. With the book called **Wisdom**, composed in the first century B.C. and disappointingly lacking in Protestant Bibles, we have "the first and only instance in the Old Testament where future life with God is categorically and clearly affirmed as man's real destiny."[3] This may seem surprising because of the prevalence of such a belief throughout the New Testament, but it only draws attention to the startling revelation of God in Jesus Christ.

3. Brown, Fitzmyer, Murphy, eds., *The Jerome Biblical Commentary* (West Paterson, NJ: Prentice-Hall, 1968), 34:6.

It might be worth reviewing here the difference between Catholic and Protestant Bibles. All Christian Bibles are, of course, divided into two main parts: the Old Testament and the New Testament. Both Protestant and Catholic Bibles have the identically same New Testament of twenty-seven books. The distinction lies in the amount of books and chapter additions in the Old Testament.

The books that comprise the Old Testament took over 1000 years to be composed, from roughly 1200 B.C. to 100 B.C. And at no time either before, during, or immediately after the time of Jesus was there a definite and exclusive group of books that alone embodied the Old Testament. This means that while the New Testament was being written, there was no definite list of Old Testament books. The New Testament authors cite many different earlier books, including some that never made their way into the Old Testament that we have today: example, the Psalms of Solomon, 1–2 Esdras, and the Assumption of Moses. As scholar Raymond Brown reminds us in the above mentioned Commentary: "Jude 14 clearly cites Enoch; and while it is often stated that the author is not citing this apocryphal book as Scripture, we have no reason to suspect that Jude would have made such a distinction. Enoch was for him, as it was for some later Christian writers, a sacred book." (page 523)

It's hard to pinpoint exactly when a definite list of Old Testament books was drawn up and widely accepted. But by the end of the second or early third century A.D., the Hebrews in Palestine seemed to have had a definite grouping of twenty-four books. These twenty-four make up the Jewish Bible as we know it today. Because Christians divide the books differently (example, Samuel becomes 1 and 2 Samuel), that same twenty-four totals thirty-nine in Protestant Bibles. I say "Protestant" because Catholic Scriptures have—in addition to those thirty-nine—seven more books, bringing their Old Testament total to forty-six. How did they get there, and where did they come from? And why the difference?

During the immediate centuries before the coming of Christ, a translation was made of Old Testament writings. This Greek version is called the *Septuagint,* a term that was eventually applied to all the Greek translations of the Old Testament and even works originally written in Greek. This was, consequently, a larger group of writings than merely the twenty-four mentioned above.

Those who wrote our present day New Testament quoted, as we earlier mentioned, from this larger corpus, a nonfixed grouping of respected Jewish works. Some of these references included books unique to the Catholic Bible: Sirach, Wisdom, 1 and 2 Maccabees, and Tobit. The Church continued that custom even after the last New Testament book was completed. But since

Review and Discussion

1. When we hear the word *prophet,* we think of someone who predicts future events. Is this accurate? What precisely does *prophecy* mean in Scripture?

2. Were prophets always graced with correct moral insights?

3. Why is spiritual direction important for the discernment of spirits working within us? When we pray about important decisions to be made, how can we know whether the insights we receive are really from God?

4. How does wisdom, as it appears in Scripture, differ from morality?

5. How does the anti-wisdom of Job and Ecclesiastes actually lead us to God?

---

there was no strict and exclusive listing of Old Testament books, there was disagreement and doubt, during the subsequent history of the Church, about the truly sacred character of various books.

By the fourth century, the Western Church had finally drawn up a fixed list or "canon." But some of the books on that list continued to be doubted in favor of the shorter twenty-four book list favored by the Jews.

At the Council of Trent (1545–1563), the Catholic Church officially accepted the list it now has. Protestants had by then already excluded this broader list in favor of that twenty-four-book Jewish canon. And so it remains to this day.

Those "doubted" books are called *deuterocanonicals.* Protestants term them and a few more books *apocrypha.* There are seven, plus parts in two other books. The full books are Tobit, Judith, Wisdom, Sirach (Ecclesiasticus), Baruch (including Jeremiah's Letter), 1 and 2 Maccabees, and the sections are in Esther and Daniel. There are accepted by Catholics as full Scripture. Protestants call them "holy" books but not the same as regular Scripture. (*JBC,* 67: 21–47)

Chapter Five

Searching for the Original Text and Its Meanings

Textual Criticism

When people extol the complete inerrancy of their biblical text and in the next breath reject the contributions of biblical scholars to the same Word of God, I am sure that they never realize that it is precisely because of that scholarship that they can rest comfortably with the belief that their English text is a reliable one. (If they trust exclusively in a 1611 King James translation, they have problems. It was done from a very poor Greek text containing fourteen centuries of errors in manuscript copying. That's why the King James has gone through various revisions.)

The Bible was not written in English, or any other modern language, for that matter. It was written in Hebrew and Greek. Consequently, our Bibles are translations of the original. Problem number one: we don't have the originals any more, nor did anyone else who ever at any time made modern language translations. The closest we can come to original Old Testament works is some fragmentary scrolls written about one hundred years after the Old Testament's latest writings.

For the New Testament the oldest seems to be the John Rylands Papyrus dating from about A.D. 130 and containing part of chapter 18 from John's Gospel.

Our almost total lack of ancient Hebrew or Greek texts is due to various factors. Wars that ravaged the Holy Land probably destroyed some. Nebuchadnezzar obliterated Jerusalem in 586 B.C. Four hundred years later Antiochus Epiphanes did his best to remove all vestiges of Jewish culture and religion. And finally the

39

Romans applied the crush of their world power by again leveling the Holy City in A.D. 70.

The fragile nature of the manuscripts themselves contributed to the loss. Biblical works were done on papyrus and parchment. Papyrus is a reed plant from which sheets of writing material were made. Parchment, the prepared skins of sheep, goats, etc., would be more stable, of course, but even it has its aging limitations.

Until the invention of printing, manuscripts of the Bible were copied by hand. Scribes who down through the years made copies of earlier copies often added explanatory material to the text.

The problem faced by scholars is that these explanations were added directly to the main text instead of in the form of footnotes. Scribes made mistakes as well, such as misreading words, wrongly copying others, skipping even entire phrases, etc. We call all these additions and deletions *corruptions* because they distort what the original authors wrote.

Textual criticism works to break through these alterations in order to arrive at the genuine text. What has resulted is a Hebrew and Greek Bible that is, in the views of scholars, a close approximation to the original. There is no other writing from antiquity that compares with it.

The discrepancy between the Catholic and Protestant ending of the Lord's Prayer shows how early manuscripts varied. The Protestant "For thine is the kingdom, the power, and the glory forever. Amen" is absent from the earliest important manuscripts. This indicates it was added later for use in worship services.[1] Catholics include it in the Mass at the end of the Our Father but separated by the "Deliver us, Lord, from every evil" prayer of the priest. This recognizes the ending's ancient history but indicates as well its original separation from the Lord's Prayer.

Another example would be John 5:4. A footnote to this verse in the *New American Bible* mentions an additional sentence inserted here but found to be missing in the best manuscripts. It reads: "For (from time to time) an angel of the Lord used to come down into the pool; and the water was stirred up, so the first one to get in (after the bubbling of the water) was healed of whatever sickness he had had." The footnote then adds: "The appearance

1. John P. Kealy, C.S.Sp., *The Changing Bible* (Denville, NJ: Dimension Books, 1977), 82–83.

of the angel is probably a popular explanation of the turbulence and the healing powers attributed to it."

Many other examples can be found in Scripture. They are usually called to the reader's attention in better Bible translations by some sort of footnote similar to the above.

Words of Jesus

As regards the New Testament, now that we are so confident that we do have a genuine and faithful text, can we be certain we have the actual words spoken by Jesus?

When we read the words of Jesus in the Bible we have to keep a few things in mind. We can't take the position of the lady in an area fundamentalist Church who objected to my statement that "It's hard to know the actual words Jesus spoke." "Oh, they're certainly clear to me," she replied. "In my Bible they're all printed in red!"

The language of Jesus was Aramaic. We read his words in English. Between the original Aramaic and our American English stands the Greek the New Testament used in reporting them (Jesus spoke Aramaic—which was translated into Greek—and from Greek into English). If you don't recognize the problem, you've probably never studied a foreign language and tried to translate.

Different words can be translated different ways.[2] Furthermore, between the death-resurrection of Jesus and the writing of the first Gospel, a period of some thirty years elapsed. It is difficult, therefore, to say where we possess actual words of Jesus. We cannot say we have them in English. We cannot even say that we have them in the New Testament Greek.

2. Sometimes the same word used in different settings can help us better understand its particular meaning in a given place. What compounds problems for translators of the Hebrew Old Testament is that thousands of words are used only once!

Probably no clearer example can be given than in the institution of the Eucharist. We somehow expect that this holiest and solemnest of moments would have been very accurately remembered, but note the differences:

The Eucharist

Matt 26:26–28

"Take this and eat it," he said, "this is my body . . . for this is my blood, the blood of the covenant, to be poured out in behalf of many for the forgiveness of sins."

Mark 14:22–24

"Take this," he said, "this is my body. . . . This is my blood, the blood of the covenant, to be poured out on behalf of many."

Luke 22:19–20

"This is my body to be given up for you. Do this as a remembrance of me. . . . This cup is the new covenant in my blood, which will be shed for you."

John has no specific Eucharist account at the Last Supper, but includes teaching on the Eucharist in chapter 6.

1 Corinthians 11:24–25

"This is my body, which is for you. Do this in remembrance of me. . . . This cup is the new covenant in my blood. Do this, whenever you drink it, in remembrance of me."

But let's not forget that "The twentieth-century Christian's faith in the Eucharist does not depend on what he/she can reconstruct of the words of the historical Jesus, but rather on the words as reflected to us through the early Christian community which recorded its diverse, varied recollections of him and of his impact on them in this matter."[3]

We should always remember that all of the texts in Scripture pertaining to the Eucharist are inspired by God. There is nothing, therefore, wrong with the variety present. What it indicates is rather how God's inspiration of the Bible is not concerned with slavish

3. Joseph A. Fitzmyer, S.J., *A Christological Catechism* (Ramsey, NJ: Paulist Press, 1982), 56.

adherence to the exact words Jesus spoke but with faithfulness to what he preached. The Church has always accepted that principle, which is evident from the eighty-some different wordings for the Eucharist in liturgies of the East and West (not counting Reformed Churches). None of these is an exact reproduction of the versions in Scripture, nor was the Pius V missal version so beloved of traditionalists."[4]

It would also be good to remind ourselves that the Church's guidance (Tradition) leaves no doubt about the meaning of those words, that, by partaking, we share in the real body and blood of Jesus.

Specific Words

However, there are instances of words ascribed to Jesus that, for various reasons, scholars feel certain are authentic. Jesus is quoted as saying to Peter: "Get out of my sight, you satan!" (Mark 8:33) They are such strong, harsh words to be directed toward one who was head of the apostles in the early Church. They must be authentic, for nothing else can explain their presence in the Gospels. The Church would never have presented Peter so unfavorably if the saying were not from Jesus himself.

Another example would be the two brief words of Jesus: *Amen* and *Abba*. They should be underlined in Bibles not just for their authenticity but for something else as well. It's remarkable that our knowledge of the exact wording of Jesus should be limited to practically these words alone, for they also summarize Jesus beautifully. They were remembered in their exact form because they were so revolutionary. *Amen* stresses the authority Jesus knew was his: "Amen, Amen I say to you." *Abba* is translated into our Bibles as *Father*. A more exact translation would be *Daddy*. It is a very intimate term and reflects the close relationship Jesus felt with his Father. Absolutely no Jew in his time would have dreamt of addressing God in so intimate a fashion. That's why the word just **has** to be authentic.

Sometimes the Hebrew and Greek texts contain words very hard to translate into modern languages. The New Testament Greek, for example, may capture the flavor of the original Aramaic

---

4. Pierre Loret, *The Story of the Mass* (Liguori, MO: Liguori Press, 1982, translation from original French), 11–15.

of Jesus' words, but that flavor is lost when an English translation is made.

One of the most moving examples is found in John 21:15–17. Two Greek words for love are *agape* (other-centered, condition-free love given generously to someone whether it is returned or not) and *philia* (a lesser love given for mutual profit). In the dialogue between Jesus and Peter, Jesus asks for *agape* love. Note Peter's responses as we substitute the proper Greek words for the simple English word *love* employed in the translation.

> *"Simon, son of John, do you* agape *me more than these?"*
> *"Yes, Lord," he said, "you know that I* philia *you."*
> . . . *A second time he [Jesus] put the question, "Simon, son of John, do you* agape *me?"*
> *"Yes, Lord," Peter said, "You know I* philia *you."*

Peter obviously cannot quite bring himself yet to the kind of love Jesus asks. So Jesus adjusts the third question asking if Peter can at least give him the lesser kind of love.

> *A third time Jesus asked him, "Simon, son of John, do you* philia *me?"*

Peter answers yes.

Divorce and Remarriage

The "lewd conduct is a separate case" clause of Matthew 5:31–32 on the question of divorce is an illustration of different wordings of Jesus in different Gospels causing a great deal of debate. If we go only by the English wording, Matthew seems to allow divorce if the wife has been guilty of "lewd conduct," "unchastity," "unfaithfulness."

> *"What I say to you is: everyone who divorces his wife— lewd conduct is a separate case—forces her to commit adultery."*

But when we look to the teaching of Jesus on divorce in Mark's Gospel (10:11–12), we find no such exception clause.

Scholars are convinced Mark's is the original form. The ban on divorce is total. How do we understand the difference then?

The word translated into "lewd conduct" is our key. In the Greek it's *porneia,* a word with different meanings including marriage within the forbidden degree of kinship (as in Acts 15:20). Even the Greek word for *wife* can simply mean "a woman." Furthermore, as the *Jerome Biblical Commentary* tells us: "If Matthew meant adultery, he chose a less apt word for it. *Porneia* means literally 'prostitution' and it designates unchaste conduct generally. *Mocheia . . .* means 'adultery.' " (43:38)

An additional help in our interpretation is the reminder that Matthew makes it a point in his Gospel to stress the really radical teaching of Jesus. Would he then include something extra that Jesus didn't say especially if it would lessen the power of his punch?

Taking all of this together, Matthew's apparent exception clause means something similar to the following: "Every one who sends away his woman—except in the case of concubinage—makes her commit adultery."[5] Matthew is really therefore conveying the same message as Mark: no divorce!

The Church today tries to balance this clear condemnation with a pastoral concern, as it has done with the other antitheses in Matthew 5:21–48 (anger and killing, oaths, impurity, retaliation, attitude toward enemies) that are given equal weight in Jesus' teaching. Sometimes **valid** marriages do in fact fail and partners remarry in good faith. Judging from the writings of contemporary theologians, in such cases if the second marriage is durable and truly loving, the partners can be admitted to the sacraments provided there is no scandal.

Father Sean O'Riordan, C.SS.R., Professor of Moral Theology at Rome's Alphonsianum mentions in the March 29/April 5, 1975 issue of *The Tablet:* "There is now a firmly established view that they can be admitted provided that they now show a true Christian spirit in their lives, that their present union is a stable one, and that scandal is avoided."

5. *JBC,* 43:38.

Father Bernard Haring, C.SS.R. agrees, as shown from a 1970 article in *Concilium* and in Volume 2 of his *Free and Faithful in Christ:*

> *Pastoral Theology and pastoral practice have come more and more to the conclusion that spouses who live in a second marriage—the destruction of which would be a disaster—should be admitted to the sacraments of Penance and Eucharist if they are longing sincerely for regular participation in the sacramental life of the Church, live in good faith regarding their new situation, have forgiven the wrong they have suffered, and are trying to give their children a good education.[6]*

The Fuller Sense of Scripture

Christians believe that the Old Testament led to Jesus. They have learned this in a special way from New Testament writers who found in the Old Testament many events, passages, and personages that reminded them of him. It is true that we must cautiously avoid the overindulgence of freely and uncritically reading limitless Old Testament passages as if the human authors were thinking of Jesus all the time. Today's scholarly tools can only give us certain knowledge of the literal meaning of what they wrote.

But, as we noted earlier, there are other possible meanings to Scripture in addition to what the biblical authors themselves intended. We can, for example, rightly hold that God may have intended things even if the human authors did not.

The Jerome Biblical Commentary in 71:57 speaks of this as the sensus plenior (SPlen), meaning "fuller sense," and defines it as "The deeper meaning, intended by God but not clearly intended by the human author, that is seen to exist in the words of Scripture when they are studied in the light of further revelation or of development in the understanding of revelation."

6. Bernard Haring, C.SS.R., *Free and Faithful in Christ,* vol. 2 (New York: Seabury Press, a Crossroads Book, 1979), 543. In *Code, Community, Ministry,* a commentary on the new Code by the Canon Law Society of America, there is an "addenda": Before one resorts to this *internal forum* solution "there is a presumption that the ordinary means of reconciliation in the external forum have been exhausted; i.e., the possibilities of declaration of nullity or dissolution of the previous marriage have been investigated and found not to exist or to be morally impossible." (Washington, DC: Canon Law Society of America, 1983), 109.

Scholars disagree on the frequency that SPlen's can be found in the Bible. Many think they are rare and, as a consequence, don't speak about them anymore. The *JBC* (71:59) mentions Matthew's statement in Matthew 1:23 that Mary's virginal conception of Jesus was the fulfillment of Isaiah's prophecy (Isaiah 7:14): "Behold, a virgin shall conceive and bear a son, and his name shall be called Emmanuel."

Our first caution comes from realizing that Isaiah's word, which we translate as *virgin,* in the original Hebrew really means simply a young woman of marriageable age. Nothing is implied about virginity. The entire context of the Isaiah text indicates the son referred to is really the child Hezekiah to be born in 734 B.C. who will continue the promised David dynasty.[7] Is Matthew's use of this quote then merely an "accommodation," a loose association, a sense he adds for the sake of devotional reflection by his audience? Or is this a genuine example of a "fuller sense" found in the original Isaiah text?

When the author of Matthew's Gospel says something similar to "This was to fulfill what had been said through the prophet," and then quotes an Old Testament text, we should not therefore automatically think a fuller sense of that passage, a further meaning intended by God, was present then. It may have been, but then again it may not have been. We simply cannot be certain.

The Typical Sense of Scripture

The *JBC* defines typical sense as "the deeper meaning that the things (persons, places and events) of Scripture possess because, according to the intention of the divine author, they foreshadow future things." (71:72)

While the "fuller sense" of Scripture dealt with the words, the "typical sense" concentrates on persons, places, and events of the Old Testament in trying to see a hidden symbolism for New Testament realities.

---

7. We must remember, in relation to all the prophets of the Old Testament, that they were "men of their time" in more ways than one. Their writings were concerned with their own day and an immediate future that they could recognize because of the way things were developing. Modern biblical scholarship denies that they had any knowledge of the far distant Christian era.

One of the classic images for the risen Christ is a lamb. The sprinkling of a lamb's blood on their doorposts caused the angel of death to "pass over" the Israelites prior to their journey from Egypt. The sacrificial lamb was a "type" of Jesus whose blood was shed to save us. John uses the Paschal Lamb theme for Jesus in different places in his Gospel.

Another example is the bronze serpent set up by Moses so that whenever "anyone who had been bitten by a serpent looked at the bronze serpent, he recovered." (Numbers 21:9) In John 3:14 Jesus refers to this as a type of himself:

> *Just as Moses lifted up the serpent in the desert, so must the Son of Man be lifted up, that all who believe may have eternal life.*

This "spiritual sense" of Scripture has, therefore, a validity from its use by Scripture itself. We have to be cautious, however, of excessive application of such typology when references are not found in the Bible (or as *JBC* 71:76 states, don't have a "*consensus* of the Fathers, of liturgical usages, and of Church documents"). This can do an injustice to an appreciation of the Old Testament's individuality.[8]

In summary, modern biblical scholarship differs on the extent to which further meanings than the author's intent can be given to Scripture. Brown notes that many scholars prefer to draw a line on the additional meaning a book received when it was officially added to the canon or approved list of biblical books in the fourth century.

Brown himself believes, however, that the door to further biblical meanings is not closed with the literal and canonical sense of books. In fact, it's flung wide open! The Church in its reflection can come to many meanings for the enrichment of the faithful, meanings which are also truly biblical. As quoted earlier, "the way in which the Church in its life, liturgy, and theology comes to understand the Bible is constitutive of 'biblical meaning' because it

---

8. St. Ambrose in his treatise, "On the Mysteries," speaks of Baptism: "Marah was a spring of bitter water. When Moses threw wood into it, its water became sweet. Water, you see, is of no avail for future salvation without the proclamation of the cross." (Cf. Breviary reading for Tuesday of the fifteenth week of the year.) Such frequent examples in Church writings are better called devotional accommodations.

is chiefly in such a context that this collection is serving as the Bible for believers."[9]

This insight is very appealing because it shows how dynamic the Bible can be. It is anything but a twentieth century irrelevancy, a story of a people of long ago with no meaning for our lives. God truly speaks in love and care to His people today.

The "truth" of Scripture should be seen as a broad and gradual enlightenment that proceeds and develops down through history. All truth is found in Jesus Christ, but it will take us an eternity to fathom the depths of who and what he is.

Review and Discussion

1. Why is it so difficult to produce a perfect modern language version of the original Bible text?

2. Why do the Catholic and Protestant versions of the Lord's Prayer differ in their endings?

3. Can you explain why the words of Jesus are reported differently in the various Gospels?

4. Comment on the teaching of Jesus about divorce. Under what conditions can divorced individuals be admitted to the sacraments?

5. Explain different meanings (literal, typical, fuller) that can be given to Scripture passages.

9. Brown, *Critical Meaning*, 34.

Chapter Six

The Fundamentalist Challenge

On a color-coded map of the United States published in 1971 by Glenmary Research Center, Webster County in West Virginia rode like a green bubble on a red sea. Green indicated we were predominantly Methodist in Church affiliation, but on the county's southern boundary began the immense red region of the Bible Belt with its characteristic Baptist faith.

The 1980 census reported a change. Webster County had been absorbed by that red sea, with almost 1700 people claiming Baptist affiliation. Catholics numbered 120, but Catholics who practiced were a measly seventy-three in a total county population of a little over 12,000. That made us in the neighborhood of .5 of one percent of the population.

There are today a great many Churches in that county, a good portion of which are nondenominational. My only source of information on the exact number of Churches came from a local minister who wanted to challenge all county ministers to a public debate on baptizing children. He stated that he had contacted forty-two ministers and sixty-five Churches (and two-thirds of the population doesn't even attend church!)

Bible fundamentalism abounds. In 1977, I began a series of weekly articles in the county paper, the *Webster Echo,* dealing with new biblical insights. My introductory remarks brought this response from a fundamentalist minister formerly from the town: "There are pagans, atheists, and infidels who call themselves Christian. Some of these even call themselves 'Reverend.' These religious wolves in sheep's clothing show themselves to be anti-Christ, for they attack the very words of Christ. . . . Why would man seek to destroy the credibility of the Bible? Because, friends, the Holy Bible condemns his ungodliness and false doctrines."

Pretty strong words! Perhaps I could only blame myself for coming on too strong, too fast. Perhaps, therefore, the fault was in large part my own.

But since that minister's response, I have become aware of a sizeable amount of anti-Catholic belief and rhetoric throughout our entire area and even our country at large. Much of it seems to be plain religious bigotry that will probably always exist.

However, a good portion of the prejudice against Catholicism seems to have a different basis. Perhaps we could call it "more honest" prejudice since it is a natural result of a manner of approaching Scripture widely present in otherwise committed Christian Churches. I have come across examples of it time and time again in my work in the mountains of central Appalachia. Some of this prejudice comes from a way of reading the book of Revelation that leads believers to see today's Roman Catholic Church as tied in eventually with the Antichrist (see footnote 1, page 118). The way these people have traditionally misunderstood Catholic beliefs, or the way, for example, a given Catholic belief seems to them to contradict something in Scripture, adds to the problem. For Scripture is their only traditionally accepted guide to things spiritual.

Their beliefs and arguments seem to be consistently based on the English wording of the Bible, and the English wording of one version, the King James. In fact, instead of applying the belief of inerrancy (protection from error) to the original biblical manuscripts, they mistakenly apply it to this one English translation.

While it may be true that at least some groups of fundamentalists "officially" apply inerrancy to the original Hebrew and Greek biblical texts and reject a view of inspiration (God's guidance) that implies a divine dictation to the human author's brain, my personal experience with fundamentalists shows something quite different. I find that the everyday adherents of fundamentalism do indeed speak and write as if the King James Bible were the only acceptable Bible translation that is faithful to God's revelation. They will use no other. And in addition they reflect an understanding of inspiration that is very much akin to a stenographic dictation.

An evangelist recently took me to task on the question of the "brothers and sisters" of Jesus. I had written an article in our county paper claiming that the scriptural evidence, when closely examined, leaves us with an unresolved problem. But for Catholics, I continued, Tradition comes to the rescue teaching us that Mary had but one child, Jesus.

The evangelist answered by reminding me that since the Bible says Jesus was Mary's "first-born son" she definitely had others. He said this was supported by the word "till" (Jospeh "knew her not **till** she had brought forth . . ."), indicating Joseph thereafter **did** know her.[1] Therefore, he continued, "You Catholics should stop glorifying Mary with the fourth century Roman Catholic doctrine of the perpetual virginity."

In this example, as in many other of their arguments, there is no reflection of any understanding of or acquaintance with scriptural scholarship,[2] of how doctrinal expressions were historically a response to a belief of the Church that was challenged, or how English translations fail to capture often the true sense of the original biblical languages.

It is this latter form of prejudice, the "more honest" type that has led me to this book. It has shown me why the Catholic Church makes smaller inroads than it should, particularly below the Mason-Dixon line where fundamentalism is so strongly entrenched. It has helped me see how deep indeed mistrust of Catholicism can be in very simple God-loving people. And it has therefore urged me to do what I can to alleviate the problem by (1) acquainting our Church at large to the real challenge evangelization and ecumenism face from this fundamentalist reading of God's Word, (2) instructing our Catholic people in proper scriptural interpretation so that they will not be influenced by their fundamentalist neighbors with whom they may be often sharing in scriptural discussion groups, and (3) challenging our Church

1. The fallacy of such a method of argumentation is shown by what the word translated as "till" means in the original Greek and other Semitic languages. It simply stresses what did not happen up to the birth of Jesus. It doesn't imply what happened afterwards. A similar expression can be found in the King James version of 2 Samuel 6:23: "Therefore, Michal the daughter of Saul had no child unto (till) the day of her death."

2. See *Mary in the New Testament,* edited by Brown, Danfried, Fitzmyer, and Reumann (Ramsey, NJ: Paulist Press, 1978). The treatment of brothers and sisters of Jesus is a good overall view of contemporary biblical insight into the question.

leaders and people to make strenuous efforts to widely share this proper scriptural interpretation through all available media so as to reach and educate anyone who will listen!

What Is Fundamentalism?

What precisely is fundamentalism, and why does it hold the allegiance of an estimated 30 percent of adult Americans?[3]

The *Oxford English Dictionary* defines fundamentalism as "a religious movement which became active among various Protestant bodies in the U.S. after the war of 1914–18, based on strict adherence to traditional orthodox tenets (e.g., the literal inerrancy of Scripture) held to be fundamental to the Christian faith; opposed to liberalism and modernism."

The *Random House College Dictionary* zeroes in on the Scriptural approach of fundamentalism: "A movement in American Protestantism that arose in the early part of the twentieth century and that stresses the infallibility of the Bible in all matters of faith and doctrine, accepting it as a literal historical record."

Thus, while fundamentalism reaches beyond merely the pages of Scripture, the Bible is its main area of concentration. In the words of Rev. Jerry Falwell, probably fundamentalism's chief public exponent, fundamentalists "see themselves as the militant and faithful defenders of biblical orthodoxy."

In their reading of Scripture, dyed-in-the-wool fundamentalists take the words at face value according to their literalistic meaning. As a result, there can be no such thing as historical, scientific, and certainly not religious error. There is no need for interpretation of the biblical texts. Everyone should be able to grasp the meanings clearly. Scriptural scholarship, rather than aiding our understanding of the Bible, destroys that understanding by watering down the impact of the message.

---

3. See the article by Father Leonard Foley, OFM, in the July, 1983, issue of *St. Anthony Messenger*. See also the lengthy, detailed, and informative article on Jerry Falwell and fundamentalism entitled "A Reporter at Large" by Frances FitzGerald in *The New Yorker* (May 18, 1981).

Areas of Difficulty

A great many reflective Christians take serious issue with this literalistic understanding of God's Word. They feel it does an extreme injustice to what God, and the human authors really wanted to say to us through Sacred Scripture. And they view with discouragement how such an interpretation of the Bible causes unwarranted tension with the findings of contemporary science.

Because of their adherence to a literalistic reading of Genesis 1–11, in which the creation of the world and humankind is symbolically described, fundamentalists are also termed "creation-science" advocates. They have been putting a tremendous amount of pressure on school boards throughout the country to include the teaching of Genesis 1–11 as genuine science, i.e., to teach the literalistic interpretation of Genesis in place of, or at least alongside of, the theory of evolution. As a result, children are being taught to accept instead of, or together with, hard scientific facts and reliable scientific theories an explanation of the world's and humankind's origins that is scientifically naive, to say the least. A little thought can help us see what results. Many children, not wanting to deny God's Word, are—to the detriment of their education—coming to hold science as suspect. Later, of course, when they do become acquainted with the truthfulness of these scientific insights, they will be strongly tempted to reject religion as irrelevant! Religion suffers and science suffers.

In the light of the sad state of public education in the United States, as documented by the 1983 report of the National Commission on Education, can school boards, teachers, and parents really afford to approve classroom materials that disparage valid scientific knowledge?

The harm that results from fundamentalism is not limited to the call for such curriculum changes in public education. With growing frequency there have been news reports of children being allowed to die from easily curable illnesses while their parents denied them medical treatment because of fundamentalist beliefs. Recent newspapers carried the story of a six-week-old Syracuse, Indiana, boy who died from acute suppurative meningitis that resulted from a small infection. His parents were "confirmed members" of Faith Assembly, a strict fundamentalist sect that requires total reliance on prayer for healing and considers the consulting of doctors an "unpardonable sin."

The death rate in West Virginia's snake-handling has risen with the growth of fundamentalism.[4] Basing their belief on a literalistic face-value reading of Mark 16:18 which states that the followers of Jesus "will be able to handle serpents . . . to drink deadly poison without harm," these fundamentalists tempt the otherwise infinite patience of God. Ministers speak of some being bitten dozens of times and of others who have not recovered. One minister tells of his mother-in-law who died after drinking strychnine at an Elk River service.

The Attraction of Fundamentalism

Why are the fundamentalist ranks swelling so rapidly? The main reason frequently given, and probably quite correctly, is the need for security. Many props have been pulled out from cherished traditional beliefs about both religion and cultural values. In our own Catholic Church, strain is felt from the changes initiated by Vatican II. Conservatives protest that too much was done too fast, while liberals counter that too little was done too slowly. Many in the liberal camp seem, as a consequence, to have either left the established Church altogether or chosen a new style of life that enables them to practice forms of "selective" Catholicism. They retain membership in the Church, faithful to established practice for the most part, but selectively choose elements of belief they can personally accept instead of "buying the whole package."

There are probably a good many conservatives who have also abandoned the Church completely as a result of all the changes. Together with the middle-of-the-roaders, many more have remained while quietly (and not so quietly, as can be seen from the ultra-conservative press) expressing dissatisfaction with new ideas and practices.

But there are signs that goodly numbers of conservative-minded Catholics have gravitated toward the fundamentalist camp. While, admittedly, it is hard to come up with accurate estimates, one magazine, *Christianity Today,* claims there are four million Catholic evangelicals. And evangelicals are noted for their fundamentalist brand of scriptural interpretation. While all Catholics

4. Although illegal in surrounding states, serpent handling has to date not been outlawed in West Virginia. These cults insist that they would continue even if it were.

who view "The 700 Club" (15 percent of its audience) or Jimmy Swaggart are not necessarily full-fledged fundamentalists, it is probably true that, by and large, they identify quite strongly with "black and white" stances on Christian issues advocated by fundamentalism.

A short time ago a letter to the editor in *Our Sunday Visitor* reflected the chagrin of a Las Cruces, New Mexico, man over the inroads fundamentalism had made in his family. He laid the blame at the feet of the Catholic Charismatic movement. He wrote: "A few years ago my niece attended the Catholic Charismatic convention at the University of Notre Dame in Indiana. She subsequently became disenchanted with the Church and embraced Protestantism. Today, with twelve years of Catholic education, she is an avowed Protestant and a member of the Assembly of God Church. So much for Charismatic Catholicism. . . . She is the first Protestant in our family since we were converted to Catholicism by Ss. Cyril and Methodius more than 1000 years ago."

In our latest family reunion, I found no less than three charismatic Catholics among my cousins in attendance. All three professed scriptural fundamentalism. And when I informed one of them of how the Catholic Church looks with disfavor on that brand of scriptural interpretation, he politely countered: "Yes, and that's why the charismatic renewal is the only hope for the Church."

While I praise God for a form of Christian worship that extols the Spirit's presence to His people, I bristle when that laudatory devotion is made one with a biblical fundamentalism that is downright misleading. It is important that the Catholic Charismatic renewal not bypass the solid foundational support of an educated Bible perspective.[5]

The questioning of so many values that were always, it seemed, taken for granted, produces a great deal of uneasiness in people today. Groups in mainline Churches that are viewed as giving in to abortion, homosexuality, divorce, sexual relationships outside marriage; the "too far left" positions taken by some scholars[6] and respectable leaders in Church and government; the

5. Fortunately, there are many charismatic Catholics who do hold to a very scholarly scriptural approach.
6. When left-wing commentators deny the reality of all biblical miracles, it is an excessive assumption that centrist biblical scholars could never accept. It may be necessary to remind fundamentalists, therefore, that misuse shouldn't destroy significance.

stress given by Churches to pressing social issues here and abroad that involve much controversy at times—all in their own way tend to cause many to wonder: When will it end? And instead of patiently waiting it out, they search for movements and leaders who bring back a strong feeling of solidity and comfort by promising and preaching clear-cut answers, no-giving-in stances, absolute certainty to perplexing doubts. Who wouldn't find this attractive? It's just that those better educated in the questions involved know that such simplified problem solving doesn't really solve all the issues. There are a great many gray areas that, despite our best efforts, defy total solutions. But because fundamentalism seems to offer such solutions, it attracts many adherents.

The personal attention these often smaller worship groups offer for Catholics immersed in large parishes and packed Sunday liturgies cannot be discounted as an additional strong calling card. Again, it's a question of responding to a need to belong, a form of security.

Other causes besides religious ones are at the heart of the attraction of fundamentalism. In rural areas in particular, poverty and its accompanying degradation lead people to abandon hope in life and instead opt for beliefs that promise a sure end to it all. Such beliefs are found in fundamentalism's concentration on the book of Revelation as depicting the end times when God's judgment will effectively fall on society, or the preaching of a "rapture" that will soon "catch-up" the faithful and free them.

Since the causes of fundamentalism are numerous, responses must also be multifaceted. It is not enough, for example, to oppose their efforts to bring their literalistic understanding of Genesis into public school classrooms. The root causes of their adverse living conditions must be met with the overcoming power of the social gospel. We cannot simply lecture to an empty stomach or an empty life. We have to bring more than the fullness of knowledge. We must bring about social justice.

But education is still critically important. Somehow we must find ways to reach fundamentalists in order to open them to a different way of understanding God's Word.

In all such efforts, we can never forget how sincere fundamentalists are. And we must always respect them for that sincerity.

They truly, before God, believe in the correctness of their convictions. Somehow we must reach them and help them change by retaining that respect.

But when all is said and done, it still remains a fact that other Christians, Catholic and Protestant alike, would be less than honest if they pretended these fundamentalist brothers and sisters of theirs were a total comfort.

Fundamentalists and Science

A fundamentalist's approach to Genesis causes probably the most consternation. His view of biblical faith directs that any admittance of scientific error in Genesis is, at the ultimate least, a gross act of unfaithfulness to God. How can error be found in God's Word, for He is ultimate truth! Those Scripture scholars, in particular, who point out contradictions, errors, and inconsistencies with the discoveries of the world of science are considered "destroyers of God's Word" or "unbelievers." Those who remain "loyal" are grouped affectionately in the term "Bible-believing Christians."

God is the author of all truth, religious and scientific. Valid observations and discoveries in either field cannot be in opposition to the other. Seeming contradictions need further analysis to see which understanding requires revision.

No attempt to canonize science is being made here. But the development of such things as nuclear weaponry and elements for biological warfare should not blind us to the beautiful truths about our created world that this same scientific field presents to us. How discoveries are used should not prevent us from honoring the field of human endeavor that is responsible for the discoveries.

And yet, isn't that what some fundamentalists do? No matter what proofs are brought forth, they must somehow question those proofs if they contradict what a literalistic "face value" scriptural reading indicates. They will always, with great sincerity, offer an alternative method of interpreting the scientific data. If the Bible says it, these fundamentalist brothers and sisters of ours believe it has got to be true. There is almost no room for interpretation of the biblical text.

Darwin and Evolution

Advocates of this scriptural fundamentalism extol scholarly writings that seem to offer support for their position. This is why we find certain Christian magazines enthusiastically disseminating views of scholars who offer corrections to aspects of evolutionary theory. These views are presented as indications that evolution is being debunked in the field of science.

But it is only to be expected that Darwin's theory of evolution will have difficulties. We're dealing with an explanation of happenings shrouded in millions of years of history. One cannot expect to find the same type of proof as one might find in currently observable phenomenon. What fundamentalists fail to recognize is that these problems with certain aspects of his theory of evolution do nothing to invalidate evolution itself.

What is being criticized by scientists is **not** the theory of evolution **per se**, but Darwin's postulate of "natural selection" of the fittest. He was convinced that the various life forms evolved one from another (e.g., fish into amphibians into reptiles into birds, etc.), and that this process happened slowly with improvements resulting from natural selection of the fittest. But gaps in the fossil records challenge that gradual progression. Consequently, another group of evolutionists sees the evolutionary process as one of "punctuated equilibrium." That is, long periods of stability were followed by sudden changes. Rare chromosomal rearrangements came about because of new diets and climates that resulted from major disasters of nature. New species were thus produced rather suddenly.

To repeat: such questioning of scientists is not a challenge to evolution. Evolution itself is a virtual certainty. What they do question is the precise **how** of it all.

In 1982, on the 100th anniversary of the death of Charles Darwin, paleontologists, geneticists, molecular biologists, and other science experts met at the Pontifical Academy of Sciences in the Vatican.[7] The Academy issued the following statement on that occasion: "We freely acknowledge that there is room for differences of opinion on such problems as species formation and the mechanisms of evolutionary change. Nonetheless, we are convinced that masses of evidence render the application of the concept of evolution to man and other primates beyond serious dispute."

Fundamentalists and Inspiration

Christian fundamentalists bring to a focal point the question of biblical inspiration. By their insistence that each and every word of the Bible "tells it like it really is," with no possibility of error scientifically, historically, and most certainly not religiously, they place themselves at odds with the majority of "mainline" Catholic and Protestant Christians.

The heart of the question of biblical inspiration that separates fundamentalists from other interpreters of Scripture is the place of human authors in the writing process. Both groups recognize the Bible as God's Word. They differ on **how** it is God's Word.

Central to the belief of many fundamentalists is what can be called the human writer's "stenographic" authorship. He is merely a tool used by God, an object taken hold of for the physical act of writing letters and words. God does all the thinking, all the composing.

The trouble with this view is that it does not account for the variance between well-written and admittedly poorly written books. Any serious reader instinctively notices this difference. Some books move us almost to tears, whereas, others make the reading process pure labor. A comparison of Isaiah (well-written)

---

7. Most Catholics probably know little if anything about this Academy. It currently consists of seventy scientists, twenty-four of whom are Nobel laureates, from twenty-five nations. They are elected by their science peers and often invite even additional experts for specialized consultation in their regularly held meetings. No one is excluded because of nationality, race, or creed. Of particular interest are the efforts they undertook after a meeting in December, 1982, dealing with the aftermath of nuclear world war. They visited heads of government in Britain, France, Russia, and the United States. Brezhnez, they reported, gave a cordial reception, but Reagan didn't even let them sit down during the ten minute encounter.

with Chronicles (terrible) serves to prove the point. Does God have good and bad days?

Obvious errors are another challenge to the approach of fundamentalism. People are listed who never really existed. In Esther, the biblical personages Queen Vashti and heroine Esther cannot be reconciled with historical documents of that period. Amestris is the real queen and spouse of Xerxes. Scientific descriptions are naive to modern minds, totally out of line with what we know today. Religious beliefs are not merely insufficient but downright erroneous. Job 14 and Sirach 14:16–17, 17:22–23 clearly deny an afterlife. "It is not that the respective authors were ignorant of the possibility of an afterlife; they brought it up as a solution and rejected it at the same time that other biblical authors were accepting it."[8]

How can such errors be reconciled with the belief of fundamentalists that God alone is wholly responsible for Scripture?

Our discussion of the contextualist method of interpretation in an earlier chapter showed how contemporary scholars prefer to deal with these difficulties. Their approach takes seriously the often flawed and very limited human element involved in the writing of the Bible. Mistakes in history, for example, are part of the author's limited knowledge and cause no problem with the real meaning and intent of God's guiding inspiration.

Some Additional Problem Texts

The following list is a further sampling of problem texts that occur frequently in Scripture and to which fundamentalists seem oblivious.

1. Hares chewing the cud? Deuteronomy 14:7 mistakenly includes the hare (rabbit family) among animals that chew the cud, a clear example of an unscientific view based merely on what "meets the eye." Its mouth's movements are misleading, however; therefore, in this instance, what the ancients saw of the universe with naked eye and included in Scripture proved to be untrue.

2. Saul's manner of death. Did Saul kill himself, or was he killed by an attendant?

8. Brown, *Critical Meaning*, 16.

In 1 Samuel 31:4, the Bible reports:

Then Saul said to his armor-bearer, "Draw your sword and run me through. . . ." But his armor-bearer, badly frightened, refused to do so. So Saul took his own sword and fell on it. *(See also 1 Chronicles 10:4)*

But in Judges 9:54 we find:

He immediately called his armor-bearer and said to him: "Draw your sword and dispatch me, lest they say of me that a woman killed me." So his attendant ran him through and he died. *(See also 2 Samuel 1:10)*

Which is correct?

Contextualist solution: We are provided with two separate traditions about the manner of Saul's death. The biblical authors simply report the traditions without making any judgment about which is correct. This same solution can be applied to the next three selections.

3. **Who killed Goliath?** 1 Samuel 17:1–51 says David performed the wonder. But 2 Samuel 21:19 says a man named Elhanan did it. 1 Chronicles 20:5 sees the problem and tries to reconcile the difference by saying Elhanan killed a **brother** of Goliath. We may well wonder if this famous action of David was really carried out by one of his brave soldiers and later merely attributed to David.

4. **Clearing the temple**. John relates that Jesus drove the sellers out of the temple at the **beginning** of his public ministry (John 2:13–17). The Synoptic Gospels say it happened at the **end** of his ministry (Matthew 21:12–13, Mark 11:15–17, Luke 19:45–46).

5. **The blind beggar**. According to Mark, Jesus heals Bartimaeus, the blind beggar, while **leaving** Jericho (Mark 10:46). Luke tells us Jesus healed the beggar while **approaching** Jericho (Luke 18:35). Luke fails to mention the beggar's name, but since he—like Mark—has only one such blind beggar incident and both relate him to Jericho, the man is obviously the same.

6. **Date of the Last Supper**. The Synoptic Gospels indicate that the Last Supper meal Jesus shared with his disciples was the official Jewish Passover meal eaten on fifteenth Nisan (cf. Mark 14:12). John, on the contrary, states that the Last Supper occurred

on the day **before** the Passover, fourteenth Nisan (John 18:28). Which is correct?

Contextualist solution: For differing reasons, John's statement is correct. Jesus shared a last meal Thursday evening that imitated details of the annual Passover meal. His intent was to show how the Eucharist was connected to the famous Jewish Passover/deliverance from Egypt. To the Synoptics, a meal with Passover features became the Passover meal itself. Theology was more important to them than proper dating.[9]

7. **Jesus misquoting Scripture**.

Mark 2:26 quotes Jesus saying how David "entered God's house in the days of *Abiathar* the high priest and ate the holy bread. . . ." The incident is reported in 1 Samuel 21:1–6, but the high priest is *Ahimelech.*

Contextualist solution: Either the evangelist misquotes Jesus and thus makes the mistake himself, or Jesus unwittingly showed a flaw in his own memory of Scripture. As St. Cyril of Alexandria reminded us: "We have admired his goodness in that for love of us he has not refused to descend to such a low position as to bear all that belongs to our nature, *included in which is ignorance."*

Matthew 23:35 again quotes Jesus: ". . . until retribution overtakes you for all the blood of the just ones shed on earth, from the blood of holy Abel to the blood of Zechariah son of *Barachiah,* whom you murdered between the temple building and the altar." However, 2 Chronicles 24:20–22, in telling us of this 825 B.C. crime, names *Jehoida* as Zechariah's father. Luke's version of the same statement of Jesus shows an awareness of the discrepancy because the phrase "son of Barachiah" is avoided.

Contextualist solution: Same as above. The other mistake Jesus makes is that he seems to consider Abel a true historical personage. The story of Cain and Abel is part of the prehistory section of Genesis. Material in those early chapters is considered by scholars to be mythical. Jesus seems to be merely reflecting the mistaken notions of his uncritical day.

9. Raymond E. Brown, "The Date of the Last Supper," *The Bible Today Reader* (Collegeville, MN: Liturgical Press, 1973): 322–328.

Making Scripture "Divine"

A fundamentalist literal interpretation also tends to divinize the words of Scripture. It implies that the **way** truths about God are written there captures the entire truth about Him. It makes God conform to a limited human language of expressing Him, instead of leaving God free to continually challenge our always somewhat deficient modes of expression.

We must instead realize that the revelation of God in history is always an **event**. He doesn't simply drop written propositions from clouds and ask that they be contained in the pages of Scripture. He acts in history, and human minds reflecting on those God-events try to describe them. God guides the descriptions so that they are essentially faithful to the meaning in the revealed event. But there can still be further descriptions of those same events. **Words have all the limitations that human life has. Nothing is absolute, complete truth, except God. The Bible faithfully captures the essential truths, but in no way exhausts them.**

When we confuse the "fullness of truth" (which is present in God) with the truths **about** God that are conveyed in the limited human words of Scripture, then Scripture hides what it is meant to illuminate. It stands in the way of God because it sets up a barrier to further understanding of Him. It substitutes for the Almighty what is really only a pale reflection of Him.

Missing the "Mystery" of God

This divinizing of God's Word also implicitly denies the mystery of God. It is interesting to note that the Bible's alpha and omega, its beginning and end, involves deeply symbolic works: Genesis 1–11 and Revelation. That symbolism has the inherent ability to convey mystery. It is almost as if God were acting the part of the master pedagogue. Many years ago I learned that when teaching something to a class, a good pedagogic approach is to tell students what you are going to say, say it, and finish by telling them what you have said. Put more simply: introduce, explain, summarize. The deeply symbolic pages of both Genesis 1–11 and Revelation, placed as they are in the introductory and summary positions of the biblical books, seem therefore to be God's way of saying to all who venture to read what comes in between: "I am mystery! No matter what you say about Me, I am always more unlike than like your descriptions!"

God would also seem to be providing us with a lesson on interpretation. Symbols, of course, have more meaning than simply their face value. Genesis and Revelation, therefore, remind us that all the pages of Scripture should be approached in an other than fundamentalist manner. There will be, as indicated in a previous chapter, folklore, parable, historical novel, and forms of literature that defy all effort to categorize. Readers who miss that lesson fail to properly understand His message in those pages.

The next two chapters of this book are devoted to a commentary on two biblical selections: Genesis 1–11 and Revelation. They comprise the opening and closing doors of the Bible, its literary alpha and omega, beginning and end. Fundamentalists concentrate on them a great deal. Rev. Tim LaHaye, a leading fundamentalist spokesman and one of the founders of the Moral Majority has stated: "The book of Genesis is really a very crucial book. Either Genesis is true or it isn't true. And if it isn't true, then you can't rely on anything in the Bible."

Revelation provides the material for a great many of their beliefs about current world history and the end times. It is the main character in their biblical prophecy arsenal. Together with Genesis it serves as the front line force in fundamentalism's attack on scriptural scholarship. They have used the media widely to disseminate their views. Consequently many Catholics have probably been strongly influenced and have little if any idea of a proper understanding of Genesis and Revelation. It is hoped that a careful reading of what follows will help to change that.

Review and Discussion

1. Can you think of several examples that show how English translations can fail to capture the true sense of the original biblical languages?

2. From your own personal experience, how would you define a *fundamentalist?*

3. Give some examples of fundamentalism outside Christianity.

4. Can you recall from the news media some examples of the danger of fundamentalist beliefs?

5. Why are so many Catholics attracted to fundamentalism?

6. What aspects of evolution have come under question by reputable secular scientists?

7. Can you think of examples from Scripture, other than these mentioned in our text, that should cause problems for fundamentalists?

8. Explain how Scripture can take the place of God instead of leading us to Him.

Chapter Seven

Genesis 1–11

A Unique Type of History

In Genesis 1–11, instead of a "Way It Occurred," we are presented with a "That It Occurred" history. Although both are valid ways of presenting history, their differences of approach are enormous. "Way It Occurred" histories are the type written today. They try to accurately detail, in an eyewitness-reporter fashion, exactly what took place. They also present us with reasons behind what occurred, but their validity as histories rests a great deal on their faithfulness to exact chronological details.

The stories of Adam and Eve, Cain and Abel, the Tower of Babel, Noah and the Ark are not historical, photographically verifiable events. Instead, they are myths, folklore used to describe religious beliefs of the Israelite authors. **That** God created, **that** He was the only one around to do the creating, **that** there were first parents, **that** they sinned, **that** sinning spread and brought punishment: Genesis 1–11 presents all these historical "facts" in symbolic myth. It is myth that cannot be equated simply with "make believe" because the truths enshrined in the myths are the truest of true.

A failure to recognize the difference in these types of history can, and unfortunately does, result in unnecessary tension between science and religion. There has been a terrible rift over Genesis, in particular. Fundamentalists insist on the reliability of the science and history contained in its pages. They refuse to admit the evolutionary insights of modern science. They miss how evolution simply tries to explain the "Way It Occurred" history approach. This has no real import for the religious message. The history of Genesis 1–11 telling us "That It Occurred" concentrates instead on the religious meaning behind creation and humankind's early experiences. Exactly how it all happened will forever elude us. But the theory of evolution probably presents us with the best general picture we'll ever get.

The Purposes of Genesis 1–11

These opening Bible chapters serve more than one function. To the Genesis authors writing in the ninth to sixth centuries B.C., history before Abraham was a mystery. In fact, if we are to accept the view of contemporary scholars about even Abraham, Isaac, and Jacob, the Israelite patriarchs, we have to admit that there is very little true history there as well. They are not a lineal grandfather-father-son relationship, as the Bible indicates. There was no real purity of blood in Jewish origins, for these three men are not even of the same ethnic background![1]

Stories about Moses, and particularly about his leading of the Israelites from Egypt, present the same difficulty of understanding what really took place. His life is filled with improbabilities and allusions to another pagan legend. No godlike Egyptian king would be such a milquetoast toward a slave population's spokesman. Perhaps one of the clearest examples of extravagant reporting (that should automatically lead us to a cautious interpretation of the Moses saga) is the number of Israelites the biblical author mentions left Egypt in the Exodus. He tells us there were 600,000 men, not counting women and children. This would give us, in all, a total exiting group of nearly three million! As McKenzie comments: ". . . one may calculate that a Hebrew host of this size would have caused an exodus of Egyptians rather than Hebrews(!)"[2]

If so little valid history can be ascribed to stories about people living from 1800 to 1200 B.C., what must we make of stories dealing with what occurred at the dawn of creation? Genesis authors were surely aware of the lack of evidence. Instead of wanting to give true history, therefore, they simply intended to create a bridge between the story of Abraham and humankind's origins.

1. See John L. McKenzie, *The Old Testament Without Illusion* (Chicago: The Thomas More Press, 1979), chapter 6.
2. McKenzie, *Old Testament,* 90.

Another of their purposes was to give an awareness of the origins of the sinfulness from which deliverance was needed. The freely composed story of Abraham begins the biblical account of salvation history, and some explanation needed to be given as to **why** such a history was necessary in the first place.

Those early chapters also serve as a good vehicle to downplay popular pagan myths of the time and clarify the erroneous beliefs contained in those myths.

Genesis: A Patchwork Quilt of Authors

Scholars have discovered four basic authorships (in addition to God) of Genesis, which they have abbreviated by the letters J, E, D, and P: Y(J)ahwist, Eloist, Deuteronomist, and Priestly. For the most part, their writings are intermingled throughout not only Genesis, but the entire Pentateuch (first five books of the Bible). Two of them are responsible for the first eleven chapters of Genesis: J and P.

We've all seen quilts made up of patch squares, each a different color. If we gave colors to these four Scripture authorships, the Pentateuch would look very much like those patchwork quilts.

For example, in the opening chapters of Genesis, P is responsible for chapters 1 and 2:1–4a; J takes over from there until chapter 5. All of that chapter is P's except verse 29, which is J's. Then J continues with chapter 6 until P steps in again in 6:9. We find the same mingling of J, E, D, and P throughout the whole Pentateuch, except for Leviticus which is totally P's.[3]

The Yahwist (J) portion was composed in the ninth century B.C., the Eloist's in the eighth century, followed by the Deuteronomist's and finally the Priestly document in the sixth century B.C. Sometime during or shortly after this same sixth century, the documents were fused into our present Pentateuch.

The religious beliefs found within the opening chapters of Genesis were presented by authors, therefore, living in the ninth to sixth centuries B.C. They "retrojected" back into stories about the world's and humankind's origins. We do not know what revelations God shared with the first humans, but whatever they were, they certainly did not come down to these Genesis authors through

3. For a color outline showing this graphically, see the one done by Rev. Eugene McAlee and included in Peter F. Ellis, *The Men and the Message of the Old Testament* (Collegeville, MN: The Liturgical Press, 1963), 57–72.

any form of tradition. We are talking about a period of more than a million years, and over such a vast amount of time faithful adherence to original traditions would be impossible to conceive. Furthermore, the ancestor of early biblical writers was Abraham, who lived in the eighteenth century B.C. In all likelihood, he was a pagan who believed originally in many gods. How could a revelation from a one God of Paradise be transmitted through pagan ancestors who believed in multiple gods? And why would God give it through the same form of creation myth found elsewhere in antiquity? Indeed, **how** could He?

What part did Moses (who lived around 1200 B.C.) play in the Pentateuch authorship? The question is important because there are many scriptural references to that authorship in both Old and New Testaments. Until the seventeenth century, it was commonly believed that he wrote everything. But vast differences of style, vocabulary, etc., made it apparent to scholars that he just couldn't have written it all. We now recognize, therefore, that Moses was the Pentateuch's author "in substance," that is, there was set in

Roadway Back Into Pre-history

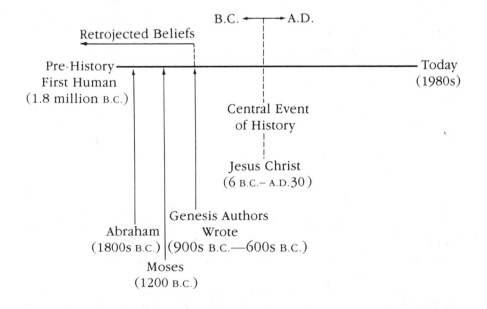

motion a long literary process that carried his influence and inspiration (as well as, of course, God's!)

Behind the J, E, D, and P authorships are, therefore, long traditions, each stressing some special aspect of divine truths.

The Creation Story of Genesis 1

Genesis begins with two quite different creation stories. The first, by a Priestly author (P)[4] who wrote in the sixth century B.C., extends from chapter 1:1 to 2:4a. His story is a deliberate attempt to counteract the popular Babylonian myths of creation with which his audience was quite familiar. Indeed, he drew on those myths as models for his writing, but replaced their paganism with the religious insights revealed to Israel.

His concepts of science are naive, to say the least. In verses 6 to 8, for example, he has God say: "Let there be a dome in the middle of the waters, to separate one body of water from the other . . . God called the dome 'the sky.' " He presents us with his scientific viewpoint of the then-known world as simply a huge body of water that God separates by placing an inverted soup bowl over a flat dish in the middle. That soup bowl dome or "firmament" kept out the waters above except to let them through "floodgates" to produce rain. God then proceeds to hang from the dome, as if from a Christmas tree, the stars, planets, sun and moon (verses 14–18). There is total ignorance of our solar system and the vastness of the universe that modern science has discovered, not the slightest intimation of the millions and billions of stars and galaxies that fill the tremendous cosmos.

This is no problem, however, except for the strict literalist. P's intention was simply to downplay the pagan notions of creation, not to teach science. Instead of imagining that the world was constructed from the dead parts of the god Tiamat after death in battle at the hands of Marduk (Babylonian creation myth), P states in no uncertain terms that God, the one and only God, created the world from nothing. In opposition to the pagan belief that the lights in the sky have divine status that determine humankind's lives, P teaches that these lights (stars and galaxies) are simply material creations of the one God of all creation.

4. He is called "Priestly" because he presents the traditions of the Jerusalem temple priests.

And when the Priestly author finally comes to the creation of man (meaning humankind), he marks him with no less an attribute than similarity to the divine: "God created man in His image" (27). Many different explanations have been offered to explain this likeness (a "physical" likeness is positively excluded!), but perhaps most appealing is the one that links "likeness" and "dominion." As in psalm 8:6–9, Genesis, verse 28, states that man will have dominion over all creatures, as does the Creator Himself. The Priestly author anticipated our present ecology and peace movements by proclaiming 2500 years ago that we must care for creation, not destroy it!

It is an exercise in futility and takes us a distant mile from the Bible author's intent to perform mental gymnastics with such things as the "six days" of creation. We impose **our** ideas, not the author's, on the text when we try to defend a literalist (fundamentalist) interpretation by claiming the "six days" could mean "six eras" or some such equivalent. That's simply missing the point.

Arranging creation into six neat days, followed by a day of rest for God, is merely a teaching device used by the Priestly author reflecting the six-day work week customary at his time. God is shown as the model workman who gives example to His people by also resting on the Sabbath.

God's "Masculinity"

The "masculinity" of God's name from the very first verses of Genesis has no real significance. Ancient myths presented gods as male and female. The Priestly author wanted to show, on the contrary, that sex was part of creation, not of divinity itself. But he couldn't use a neuter name for God because there is no neuter in Hebrew grammar. And using a feminine term would have been undesirable, because much of his culture viewed women as inferior. God as feminine would have given the impression that the author was trying to say something that he really wasn't. He was left with one final alternative: masculine.

The statement in Genesis 3:16 that the woman's husband will be her "master" is not a reflection of God's will. Chapter 3 treats of sin and its consequences. Therefore, it is because of **sin** that the husband does his "mastering." God's will for husband and wife is found in the earlier second chapter that stresses equality.

The True Science Picture

One of the most delightful tools for teaching the true age of the universe and humankind is the cosmic calendar of Dr. Carl Sagan (of TV's "Cosmos" fame). It compresses the lifetime of the universe into a single year (each month covering 1¼ billion years, each second—500 years), with the theorized "Big Bang" origin on January 1st, 15–20 billion B.C. The formation of the earth would have occurred some 10–15 billion years later, roughly on September 14th. The first human would not have arrived until December 31st, 10:30 P.M., over a million years ago, and the 500 years surrounding our time would be encompassed in that year's final second!

Another educational technique would be to imagine the world's history as enclosed in a 1000 page book, with five million years on each page. The past 10,000 years would be found in the last word!

There is no reason to pit Genesis against evolution. Each speaks of a different aspect of creation. Genesis, a religious work, gives us the theology. Evolution attempts to explain the manner. The fanciful myths used by P and the other Genesis authors are simply tools with which they communicate their religious beliefs. Scientific discoveries have given a view of the probably true manner of creation that the biblical authors could never have imagined.

Insisting on the scientific truthfulness of the Genesis creation account makes God a creator of deception: our scientific instruments tell us that star lights we now see originated millions of years ago; we continue to discover fossil records in various strata that took millions of years to form. Why would God have made these things appear this way if he **really** created everything only a few thousand years ago?

One of the clearest teachings by nature of its evolutionary past can be found in a day-long donkey ride down the Grand Canyon. The deeper one goes, the further back in time one travels. The different strata of rock formations—some the product of salt water seas, others of fresh water—exhibit ever more primitive life forms. Today's life-forms are not observable except at the highest canyon levels. It is preposterous to believe that all these strata were laid down in a single year by a relatively recent worldwide flood. Scientists, on the contrary, tell us it took many millions of years!

The *New Catholic Encyclopedia,* speaking of organic evolution in particular, reminds us:

> *Evidence from paleontology, genetics, natural selection, biogeography, taxonomy, comparative anatomy, general biology, physiology, biochemistry, embryology, and physical anthropology have been brought to bear on the problem of origins. Each in its own way converges upon and supports the general conclusion of the fact of organic evolution. The best judges of the matter are the specialists who, over a period of 100 years, have assembled the necessary evidence. For them the fact of evolution has been established as thoroughly as science can establish facts of the past not witnessed by human eyes.*[5]

After recalling how Pius XII's 1950 *Humani Generis* recognized evolution as a valid hypothesis, the *New Catholic Encyclopedia* continues:

> *Since then an increasing number of theologians have come to respect the well-documented majority opinion among scientists concerning evolutionary origins. . . . Evolutionary insights are more and more applied to theology, especially since the publication of the works of Pierre Theilhard de Chardin. In fact, the view is beginning to emerge, inverting the common opinion of the last century, that revelation says less about evolution than evolution says about the theology of creation. (page 685)*

Let us remember that "theory" in science is quite different from our everyday popular use of the term. For us, "theory" and "guess" are usually synonymous. In science, "theory" is, on the contrary, a well-organized hypothesis. In the case of evolution, it is a theory that is constantly being corroborated by mounting evidence. It has been described as *the* most important of science theories, a true bedrock of modern science. Can we really, therefore, disparage or ignore it and still call ourselves educated?

5. *New Catholic Encyclopedia,* vol. 5 (New York: McGraw-Hill, 1967), 689.

The Fertility Cult Motif

The second creation story begins with chapter 2, verse 4b. The author is called "Yahwist" (abbreviated by J because of the German spelling "Jahwist"). "Yahwist" comes from his use of the name *Yahweh* for God, a name that actually wasn't revealed until the time of Moses (Exodus 3).[6] The Yahwist wrote somewhere around the 900s B.C. Unlike the Priestly author, who stresses the almighty power of the God of all creation, J's God is the intimate friend. He walks with man and woman in the lush garden until they sin (cf. chapter 3:8).

When the Yahwist author wrote, his Israelite audience was living in the midst of the Canaanite people. The religious beliefs of these people were a constant threat to the tenets of the Israelite faith. The Canaanites were nature worshippers whose prayers and sacrifices were concerned with the fertility of their fields, flocks, and families. They worshipped many gods, especially Baal and his consort Anath. Infant sacrifice[7] and sacred prostitution were two of their worship forms. The wide extent of this "farmer's religion" can be seen in the frequency with which nude figurines and plaques of serpents have been unearthed in Palestinian excavations. Sometimes the nude figurines, symbolizing the Canaanite goddess of fertility, are found with the serpent in their hands or entwined about their bodies.

One of the main purposes of this biblical author is to counteract the influence of this pagan religion. Therefore, he uses again

6. The name revealed to Moses was the Tetragrammaton YHWH. The Israelites in later Old Testament history normally avoided pronouncing this sacred name. In its place, they would instead read "Adonai" meaning "Lord". The hybrid "Jahovah" arose from mistakenly joining YHWH and vowels of *Adonai* together (YaHoWaH). Scholars say "Yahweh" is the proper rendering.

7. Later on in Genesis 22 can be found the story of Abraham's attempt to sacrifice his son Isaac. Believing this was God's will, he made all the necessary preparations, only to be stayed in the last possible instant by an angel's protective hand. When we realize how widespread was pagan belief in human sacrifice, we can easily understand how it was possible for an Israelite patriarch to be tempted to do the same. Rather than God commanding Abraham to offer Isaac, we should instead see Abraham following what he *thought* God wanted. Being a very devout man, he would be willing to go "all the way" in serving God. The story's lesson is more than faithfulness to God's will, therefore. It is a strong command not to follow this abominable pagan religious practice.

In Judges 11:29–39, there is an incident in the life of an Israelite "judge" or "deliverer" who offered his own daughter as a holocaust to God because of a vow he erroneously made. Despite the man's conviction, there is no way God could approve of what he did.

and again the Canaanite fertility cult as a motif in his stories. Essentially he is pointing out that there is only one God, Yahweh. And therefore He alone is the God of fertility.

Adam and Eve

The Yahwist author tells us that "the Lord God formed man out of the clay of the ground" (2:7). The author was not being original when he wrote this, for we find that same creation method in other religions' myths. The mother goddess Mami, in one Babylonian text, declares: "Let him be formed out of clay, be animated with blood!" The Yahwist doesn't intend, therefore, that his description be taken as the physical way God acted to produce the first human. He was simply borrowing from another myth to teach the truth that Yahweh is the creator of the human race.

We don't find the proper name *Adam* until 4:25. Bible translations (example: King James) that use it earlier are mistaken, for they are not following the original Hebrew text correctly. Until 4:25 the Hebrew is *hā'ādām*. Since a person's name is never preceded by the definite article *(hā),* the translation should be simply "the man" or better "the human" since no maleness is suggested. The Yahwist means him to stand for all, rather than be seen as a precise individual. "The woman" is called *Eve* in 3:20 because that name resembles the Hebrew word for "life." It's not her name as much as the manner in which the Yahwist describes her origin that captures our special interest. Her creation from the side of the man indicates her equality to him, rather than any type of inferiority.

A good interpretation for the command to avoid the tree of "knowledge of good and bad" (2:17) sees "knowledge" to mean "experience" in Hebrew. It's not a mere intellectual knowing. The prohibition is against choosing what one wants with no moral restraint whatever. There is a tendency today for people to confuse freedom with anarchy. But there must be laws, there must be guidelines, if freedom is to be protected. For Adam and Eve to eat the forbidden fruit of this tree meant that they fell prey to the same confusion.

In substituting evolution as a truer description of human beginnings, we have to recognize that God did something special in making the first person, and indeed every subsequent person. We may have evolved from some lower life forms, but our spiritual power, our soul, comes uniquely from God. We are different from every other creature, and God's special intervention brought that about.

The Yahwist, in 2:20, has the man giving names to all the birds and animals. It was Hebrew belief that if you named something, you had a form of control or dominion over it. In Exodus, when Moses asks the divine name, he is given that mysterious name YHWH (which we translate Yahweh). One interpretation of the meaning of YHWH is "I am who I am." In other words, "don't try to control me by learning my name!" The man's dominion over creation that he shares with God is affirmed by the author telling us he named the animals brought before him.

Polygenism and Original Sin

Polygenism

Since the story of Adam and Eve is mythical, is it necessary to continue to believe in monogenism (i.e., that we are all descended from a single pair of ancestors)? Many scholars do not think so.

It is true that Pope Pius XII in his encyclical *Humani Generis* rejected polygenism (the belief that there were more than one pair of original ancestors) because he believed it hard to reconcile with the doctrine of original sin. But "the development of Catholic theology has advanced so far that the compatibility of polygenism and the dogma of original sin has become gradually clearer. Hence in spite of *Humani Generis,* some form of polygenism may be prudently maintained."[8] This brings theology more comfortably in line with scientific opinion which takes polygenism pretty much for granted today.

Original Sin

We should not make the mistake of believing that the doctrine of original sin is found in Genesis. It is not. However, Genesis does give us the background for the later treatment of the doctrine in 1 Corinthians 15:21ff, Romans 5:12–21, and in later Church history. The Genesis story of Adam and Eve disobediently

8. Karl Rahner, *Encyclopedia of Theology* (New York: Seabury Press, 1975), 975.

eating fruit, the immediate results of their action, and the subsequent spreading of evil through Genesis 1–11 is the symbolic material from which the doctrine takes shape.

A contemporary approach to original sin expands the traditional one. Instead of viewing original sin as a static, one-time offense that all humankind inherits, we are asked instead to view it as close to, and perhaps identical with, the "sin of the world" (John 1:29).[9] Our first parents misused their liberty. Their wrongdoing had an effect on their children who were now conceived into a sin-affected world, a disordered existence. In a series of dramatic stories, the early biblical authors describe how sin has smothered human life, causing a deterioration of the human condition. The momentum of sin, once begun, is hard to stop. Down through the centuries, that evil (continually reinforced by each subsequent member of the human race as he or she sins) all contributes to the "sin of the world." In the words of Father Haring: "We are faced with an inherited sin-tradition (Romans 5:12–21) and with a collective power of sin called by St. John the 'sin of the world' (John 1:29, cf. 1 John 2:16)." It is a state into which we are all born, for all life is shaped and conditioned by what has gone before. In fact, it works its sinister effect even during our prenatal existence. For from our first moments we lack the ability to overcome it. We need release from this bondage if we are to be saved. We cannot, unaided, free ourselves. In Baptism, we not only receive sanctifying grace (oneness with God), whereby God gives us help to overcome that evil encompassing us, but we are joined to the Church, a community of believers, that through our life will guide, sustain, and nourish that gift of grace. We are not only "gifted" but steered in the right direction.

Multiple ancestors, instead of merely one Adam and Eve, are very possible with this line of thought. For the essential truth is that, in and from our very beginnings, sin was committed. It matters not whether one pair of first parents, or different pairs, sinned. Freedom was misused. And sin, once begun, affects all who follow.

9. See Bernard Haring, *Free And Faithful In Christ,* vol. 1 (New York: Seabury Press, 1978), 129–133, 424–426. See also Monika Hellwig, *What Are The Theologians Saying?* (Dayton, OH: Pflaum Press, 1970), chapter 7.

The Serpent in the Garden

As has been noted, one of the fertility cult symbols was a serpent. Its fertility connection stems from its use, along with nude figurines of the goddess of fertility, in the Canaanite fertility cult religion. Since the Israelites were continually being seduced by this pagan religion practiced around them, the Bible writer exposes the inherent evil of the cult by making the cult's serpent symbol the tempter in the garden.

Although we usually associate Satan with the serpent tempter, this connection was not made by the biblical author of Genesis 3. The Israelites had no clear idea of Satan at the time this author wrote (ninth century B.C.). But both author and audience evidently understood the serpent as an evil symbol because of its connection not only with the forbidden Canaanite faith but also with the evil symbolism in many ancient cultures.

Revelation, the Bible's final book, speaks of the ancient serpent as Satan (20:2). The author evidently means the serpent in the garden. But we must always be careful not to put later beliefs back into the beliefs of the writers who originally wrote the stories.

Genesis 3:15 is a good example of how Christians often apply to Scripture a meaning that it originally didn't have. Not that this is something bad! On the contrary, it reminds us that the literal sense of the Bible is only one of many insights into biblical meaning. Joining each book into a wider canon of books added meaning, as does the Church today when it finds in Scripture passages important new lessons for its members' lives. As we intimated earlier, God's truth is so immeasurably rich that nothing can fully capture it!

But we should always try to understand what the biblical writer himself meant when he wrote. The author in 3:15 has God addressing the serpent: "I will put enmity between you and the woman, and between your offspring and hers; he will strike at your head while you strike at his heel." All the author is really saying is that a conflict will continue between the offspring of both. This was not a messianic text, a "protoevangelium": (beginning of the good news) of a coming redeemer. Jewish thought never interpreted it in that fashion. Christian thought did, however, seeing *he* as really referring to Christ and *you* to Satan.[10]

Cain and Abel

A careful reader should be struck by the occupations that the Bible attributes to Cain and Abel, the children of Adam and Eve, for their names are simply symbols. In Genesis 4:2 we read that "Abel became a keeper of flocks, and Cain a tiller of the soil." The Israelites were essentially shepherds or herdsmen, while the Canaanites were agrarian (farmers). Note also the similarity of name: *Cain* and *Canaanites.* It should not be difficult to see what the author has in mind.

Cain represents the Canaanites. He is cursed by God for his crime of murdering Abel (who represents the Israelites). There is enmity, therefore, between the Israelites and Cain's descendants, the Canaanites, whose religious practices are abominable. It is the author's underhanded way of again criticizing the Canaanite religion and warning his audience to beware of contacts with it.[11]

An elderly man I once knew would frequently engage me in conversation about contemporary social issues. More than once he brought up the "mark of Cain" (Genesis 4:15) as the reason behind the black skin of Afro-Americans. Such prejudicial reading of Scripture says nothing about the meaning of Bible passages but a great deal about the commentator! The Bible was simply relating a mythical origin of nomadic tatoos, marks on members of various clans that served as a protective identification ("If you harm me, my family's gonna getcha!")

The Cain and Abel story is a vehicle for an important lesson the Yahwist author wants his audience to learn about sin. Sin causes alienation. It was symbolized in the embarrassment Adam and Eve experienced because of their nakedness, an embarrassment that wasn't there before they sinned. It was symbolized also in the efforts they made to hide themselves from the God who had

10. Bruce Vawter, *On Genesis* (New York: Doubleday and Company, Inc., 1977), 83–84.
11. The message is repeated in 9:21–22. When Noah became drunk on wine, he "lay naked inside his tent. Ham, the father of Canaan, saw his father's nakedness, and he told his two brothers outside about it." When Noah later discovered Ham did not hide his shame, he cursed Ham's son Canaan (read *Canaanites*).

82

previously been, it seems, their walking companion in the garden. Now the alienation reaches a peak: it gives rise to the heinous crime of murder, and murder of one to whom a person should be tied by the closest bonds—a brother!

Genealogy and Ages in Genesis 5 and 11

When comparing these two chapters, one immediately notices that lifespans were shortening considerably. In the first genealogy, the death ages of the ten men given extend from 969 (Methusalah)[12] to 777 (Lamech). In the second list of another ten, they range from Shem (600) to the comparative early death age of Nahor at 148. James Ussher, an Irish Anglican archbishop, published his chronology of the Bible in 1650. According to his painstaking calculations, adding all such genealogies together, the spirit of God moved over the primitive waters in 4004 b.c. Some Bibles still publish his dates in their margins.

This is, however, missing the biblical author's intent. He was definitely not trying to give true chronological ages. If he was, and God was behind it, we can only suppose God was playing games with him. The earth we live on is almost five billion years old, and humanity over a million years. No, the author's intent was quite different.

First, he was imitating a literary device found in Babylonian literature. In order to indicate vast periods of time, authors would give phenomenal ages to artificial groupings of ten men.[13] Second, the author was simply using these lengthier ages in the earlier genealogy to state symbolically a belief that is found frequently in the Old Testament: a long life is a sign of sinlessness. Sin wasn't so strongly entrenched at first. The shorter lifespans in the second genealogy (which is listed after the flood) are a subtle way of showing, therefore, how the malice of sin was growing. Even the flood didn't stop the sinful tide! Once sin began (Adam and Eve's disobedience, Cain's murder), it spread its sinister influence like ripples in a previously still pond encompassing every living soul.

12. An ancient Sumerian list includes one individual who makes Methusalah's age seem pathetically insignificant. He was supposedly a king, one Emmenduranna of Sippar, whose life span totaled 72,000 years.
13. Vawter, *On Genesis,* 104.

83

A similar lesson has been voiced in our own day by the twentieth century's humble prophet Mother Teresa. Speaking at an antinuclear rally she warned: "If we are no longer concerned about love in our homes, if we can turn our backs on love, if we can kill our unborn babies, we can do anything. A nuclear holocaust would be no surprise!"

We wonder why in 5:24 an individual named Enoch is said to have "walked with God, and he was no longer here, for God took him." Several biblical themes coalesce around Enoch. "Walking with God" denotes closeness, affinity, a clear allusion to the very good life Enoch supposedly lived. His reward is really three-fold: he lived a long life himself (the symbolic 365 years); he shared in a gift granted only to the later propet Elijah, the gift of passage rather than death; and his son Methusalah was given the longest lifespan in the entire Bible, 969 years. Why the biblical author selected Enoch and attributed to him such blessings was probably merely a more forceful teaching lesson on the importance of goodness. In the midst of a genealogy reflecting the reward of many years for the relative goodness of humanity before sinning became too widespread, the mythical personage Enoch serves as a more lucid example of the theme.

Sons of God and Daughters of Men

The Yahwist's introduction to the flood story consists of a pagan myth about sexual relations between sons of god and daughters of men. At the fall festivals of the Canaanite religion, worshippers would engage in sexual relations with male and female prostitutes in imitation of the gods Baal and Anath. They hoped thereby to win the gods' favor of fertility on their crops. The biblical author disparages the myth by first of all showing that these idolatrous activities produce giants or "weirdos" ("At that time the Nephilim [giants] appeared on earth"). And then with evident humor he indicates the kind of fertility rains that result from such degrading practices: a flood that causes total destruction!

The Flood and Noah

One of the most famous popular pagan myths probably well-known to the ancient Israelites was the Gilgamesh Epic. Dating to as far back as the twentieth century B.C. (or even thirtieth century B.C., if based, as the evidence indicates, on an earlier Sumerian tale), it is perhaps the oldest story ever recorded. The hero, Gilgamesh, in his search for immortality, comes upon an old ancestor named Utnapishtim who details a great flood he survived.

It is clear when the Epic is compared with the Yahwist and Priestly authors' story of Noah's ark (composed in the ninth and sixth centuries B.C. respectively) that the Epic and the biblical tale are remarkably similar, ark and all. As examples, consider the following:

Reason for the Flood

Genesis 6:12–14. "When God saw how corrupt the earth had become, since all mortals led depraved lives on earth, he said to Noah: 'I have decided to put an end to all mortals on earth; the earth is full of lawlessness because of them.' "

Gilgamesh Epic. Several reasons are given. One document attributes it to man's sin (although the nature of the sin is not mentioned); another document fragment from the Atrahasis epic says the cause was the noise of man depriving the god Enlil of his sleep.

Preparation for the Flood

Genesis 6:14–20. "Make yourself an ark of gopherwood, put various compartments in it, and cover it inside and out with pitch. . . . But with you I will establish my covenant; you and your sons, your wife and your sons' wives, shall go into the ark. Of all other living creatures you shall bring two into the ark, one male and one female, that you may keep them alive with you."

Gilgamesh Epic, Tablet XI. "Man of Shurippak, son of Ubara-Tutu! Tear down your home and build a ship! Abandon your possessions . . . save your life. Lead into the ship the seed of all living creatures. The ship's . . . width and length shall be the same. Cover it like the underground waters."

Determining the Flood's End

Genesis 8:6–12. "At the end of forty days Noah opened the hatch he had made in the ark, and he sent out a raven, to see if the waters had lessened on the earth. It flew back and forth until the waters dried off from the earth. Then he sent out a dove, to see if the waters had lessened on the earth. But the dove could find no place to alight and perch, and it returned to him in the ark, for there was water all over the earth. . . . He waited seven days more and again sent the dove out from the ark. In the evening the dove came back to him, and there in its bill was a plucked-off olive leaf! So Noah knew that the waters had lessened on the earth. He waited still another seven days and then released the dove once more; and this time it did not come back."

Gilgamesh Epic, Tablet XI. "When the seventh day came, I released a dove and let her go. The dove went away and returned to me; there was no resting-place. . . . Then I released a swallow. . . . The swallow went away and returned to me; there was no resting-place. Then I sent forth a raven. . . . The raven went away, and when she saw that the waters had gone down, she ate, she flew about, and did not return."

Other common elements of the two stories include the ark resting on top of a mountain and, finally, the offering of a sacrifice.

The similarity of the Gilgamesh Epic and the Genesis story can be explained as either a dependence of Gilgamesh on Genesis, a dependence of Genesis on Gilgamesh, or a dependence of both upon a common ancestor. Scholars positively exclude the first (dependency of Gilgamesh on Genesis) because of the great antiquity of the Babylonian tale. And although many seem to favor the second alternative (Genesis dependency on Gilgamesh), continued difficulties with that choice make a common ancestor the more likely interpretation.

Similarities between the Gilgamesh Epic and the Genesis account show how the ancient Hebrews borrowed material from other pagan traditions and recast them to suit the telling of their own religious beliefs. There is no historical value, however, in either of these tales or in similar flood traditions of ancient peoples, for they are fraught with myths.

Therefore, the Bible version of the flood is hardly trying to teach us a true historical tale. It was only attempting to counter the pagan elements of these well-known myths. Put quite simply, there was no Noah's ark. There is possibly preserved in the stories, however, an ancient tradition of a major flood somewhere in antiquity. This is hardly surprising. Mesopotamia literally means "the land between the rivers" Tigris and Euphrates. And when a flood occurred (undoubtedly there were many), the natives considered it worldwide, for Mesopotamia was the extent of their known world. Archaeology clearly indicates that there has never been a flood covering the entire earth. The finding of shark bones atop some mountains indicates merely how earth's forces have pushed areas previously covered by water into mountainous ridges.

Fundamentalists have been trying to find evidence for the ark on top of today's Mt. Ararat. The Bible says, however, that the ark rested "on the mountains of Ararat" (8:4) in today's Armenia. No specific mountain is mentioned. Furthermore, such an attempt is merely trying to find historical truth in symbolic myth. Essentially, all the biblical author wants to teach us by the flood story is that sin causes humankind to destroy not only itself but its world as well. A nuclear age especially needs to hear this!

Noah: Drunk and Naked

Chapter 9:18–29 picks up again the anti-Canaanite motif that was evident in the story of Cain and Abel. The important clue in the story is found in the names of the three sons of Noah. Shem is the ancestor of the Semites, the people from whom the Israelites descended. Ham "was the father of Canaan," who therefore represents one of the progenitors of the hated Canaanites, while Japheth seems to be simply the ancestor of Israel's friends and neighbors who "dwell among the tents of Shem." Israelite piety would cringe at the thought of a naked father not being modestly covered by a witnessing son. Ham apparently failed to do just that, but simply told his brothers of the misfortune. As a result, Noah curses Ham's Canaanite descendants (a mythical allusion to Canaanite depravity that should be avoided by the Israelites) and praises the descendants of Shem and Japheth.

The Tower of Babel

In the story of the Tower of Babel, the author once again uses elements of pagan myths or folk legends that he alters with his Israelite beliefs.

The Tower of Babel was a ziggurat. Ziggurats were towers erected next to temples, with stairs leading to small shrines nestled on the very tops. They were thus seen as meeting places between the gods and men. Although too little is known about ziggurats to be certain, it is suspected that intercourse with sacred prostitutes may have been performed inside these shrines.

The biblical author's use of the myths to emphasize the confusion of those building the tower (symbolized by a variety of languages) is meant to be a teaching against pride, against the continual effort of humankind to decide its own destiny. The tower is presented as man's attempt to reach heaven, to be like the gods. God's wrath flows from any such forms of pride by which people try to make themselves more than they are. For in so doing, they fail to be open enough to what God alone can accomplish within them and for them. It is a mythical way of teaching our proverbial "pride before the fall."

Abraham's Ancestors

The final verses of chapter 11 are not really connected with prehistory. (Chapters and verses were not part of the Bible's original composition. It was not until the thirteenth century that biblical books were divided into chapters and not until the sixteenth century into verses.) These verses reflect the biblical attempt to link together the prehistory section with the story of Abraham that began in chapter 12. But they are not strict history either. The immediate family background of the patriarchs Abraham, Isaac, and Jacob, like the patriarchs themselves, probably reflect true historical persons. But the social class and other conflicting traditions about them lead us to be wary of any attribution of really strict, unbiased history.

An example to use in responding to the fundamentalist tendency to interpret literally even the given age of personages in Scripture can be found in Genesis 11:32 ("The lifetime of Terah was 205 years"). There is a conflict between this passage and Jewish tradition reflected in Acts 7:4 on the age of Terah. Genesis 11:26 tells us Terah was seventy when he sired Abram (Abraham). He moved his family to Haran, which Abraham left when he (Abraham) was seventy-five (Genesis 12:4). If, as Acts 7:4 states,

Abraham left Haran for Canaan *after* his father died, Terah would have been only 145!

Another version of Scripture, the Samaritan Pentateuch,[14] reflecting the same tradition expressed by Stephen, changed Genesis 11:32 from 205 to 145. Both Genesis and Acts are part of Sacred Scripture. How can a fundamentalist reading explain the contradiction if God alone, who can never err, is the sole author of Scripture?

Chapter 11 of Genesis ends, therefore, on a cautionary note. Even as it begins the important story of the ancestors of Judaism, it signals readers to beware of a too literalistic interpretation of what will follow. For it carries over a good bit of earlier mythical folklore into what should be a more historically accurate chronology of events. Readers are left, subsequently, with the same warning voiced by the beginning and ending positions occupied by the Bible's most symbolic works, Genesis and Revelation: beware a too literal approach to what comes in between!

14. This Scripture version is limited to the Pentateuch, the Bible's first five books. We are not sure of the date of its composition. Some portions can be found in the scrolls discovered at the Dead Sea community of Qumran since 1947.

Review and Discussion

1. Does Genesis belong in science class?

2. Explain the difference between "way it occurred" and "that it occurred" histories.

3. What do you believe really occurred at the Exodus from Egypt; i.e., what was the core historical event that served as the foundation for the enlarged and dramatized Scripture story?

4. Explain some differences between the two creation stories at the beginning of Genesis. In what ways are they both true?

5. Is God *male?*

6. What is the view of the Catholic Church on evolution?

7. Discuss the fertility cult motif behind Genesis.

8. Were the names of our first parents really Adam and Eve?

9. In science, is a theory the same as a guess?

10. How does Baptism take away original sin?

11. Who do Cain and Abel represent?

12. What is the meaning of the long lives ascribed to Adam and Eve's descendants?

13. Is it possible that someday planks of wood may be found atop the mountains of Ararat? If so, what would that mean?

Chapter Eight

The Book of Revelation

Perhaps no book in the Bible causes such confusion as the final book, the book of Revelation (also called the Apocalypse). The confusion stems from the book's strange symbolism and a misunderstanding of its prophetic nature. Because many people have thought that Revelation told details of the world's future, each age has had its share of interpreters who have tried to "make sense" out of it all. But, through their misguided intentions, they have only succeeded in confusing and discouraging countless believers, and have caused rifts in the unity that should grace God's people.

The Catholic Church's approach to the book of Revelation is that shared by innumerable scholars from different denominations. They see this book simply as an example of a type of literature that was present from 200 B.C. to A.D. 200 and that was written to encourage and support those undergoing persecution and suffering for their beliefs. A good deal of the symbolism is a coded reference to the persecutors, "coded" because, in this view, if the literature had explicitly profaned the persecutors and then fallen into their hands, believers could have been accused of treason.

Scholar John Randall, in his delightful little paperback entitled *The Book of Revelation,* provides a thumbnail summary that artfully captures the essence of contemporary biblical scholarship about this book.

> *The Book of Revelation is at least 95 percent concerned with the events of the first and second centuries. So instead of being a prophetic book for our times, it's a book*

mostly about past history where we might see applica-
tions and parallels and learn a good deal for ourselves.[1]

His explanation is important because of the prevailing and
very popular view today that this book refers in explicit detail to
events and nations of the twentieth century. This application to
today couldn't be further from the truth. Such a view is totally contrary to the nature of apocalyptic literature, Revelation included.
Its prophetic nature is in terms of *speaking for God* rather than
predicting the future.

Perhaps one of the greatest problems that results from misreading Revelation in this way is that such a misguided approach
makes the book fearful and disturbing. The opposite should be
true. It was written to be consoling and encouraging! The author
intends God to appear as the vindicator, the savior, who will ultimately lead the sufferers to the freedom of a new life.

The book of Revelation is like other Christian and Jewish
works written in the four-hundred-year period surrounding the
time of Christ. They are reflections on events of the times when
believers were undergoing persecution and suffering for their
faith. Like other apocalyptic works of Scripture, Revelation makes
use of end-of-time symbolism to describe what was taking place
during Christianity's first century of existence. This called attention to how God would "ultimately" balance the scales in favor
of those unjustly persecuted. The persecutors themselves are described in symbols (usually fearful symbols), and, once they are
understood properly, the books can be seen in their true light.

In Revelation the persecutor is the pagan Roman empire that
caused havoc to the nascent Church as it attempted to gain a foot-
hold in Roman lands. The events and symbols described in the
book were accomplished, for the most part, in the first two hundred
years of Christianity. The "future" predictions are future in a very
broad sense: evil and good will always be at war, but good will
eventually conquer.

Recent books, such as Hal Lindsey's *Late Great Planet Earth*
and *Countdown To Armageddon,* continue a long but sad tradition in Christianity of totally misreading the intent of both authors
of Revelation: the human and the divine! Not having understood

1. John Randall, *The Book of Revelation* (Locust Valley, NY: Living
Flame Press, 1976), 14.

this unique type of Bible literature, preachers, writers, and many of the everyday faithful have continued to view Revelation as a mysterious book prophesying the end of the world. Basing their estimates on their own private interpretations of this book, they have taken turns in guessing when the fearsome end event would occur. As each foretold "end" failed to arrive, another would-be prophet always surfaced to produce a new interpretation and a new date. Such guesswork might seem merely an innocent pastime except for the many disillusioned people left in the wakes, unfairly disillusioned about Scripture because they were led to believe its predictions were not true. How many people through history have subsequently abandoned their faith as a result of such misinterpretations? That there *will* be an end to our present world is, of course, somewhere in God's plan ("transformation" would be a better word). But the point is, no detailed outline can be found in Scripture. Attempts to provide such outlines from a book like Revelation are simply guesswork and a total misreading of the work.

Symbolism

Symbolism pervades the Bible; it is one of the mediums through which God conveys truth. The importance of symbol is not limited merely to a teaching technique for those unable to read, though that was the situation widely present in biblical times. Symbol also serves as a vehicle for expressing depth of insight into realities difficult or impossible to describe in a more literal way. Symbols "charge" not only our imaginations but our emotions and religious sensitivities as well.

As the *New Catholic Encyclopedia* (volume 13, page 862) states:

> *Symbolism derives its power from the fact that it speaks not only to the reflective intelligence but to the entire human psyche. It arouses deep emotional experience, releases hidden energies in the soul, gives strength and stability to the personality, establishes strong loyalties, and disposes a man for consistent and committed action. By reason of these properties, symbols are of great importance in art and literature (image, metaphor,*

93

etc.), in psychotherapy (e.g., dream analysis), in the cementing of human societies (e.g., the flag), and in religious worship (the icon, ritual, etc.).

Just about everything in life can be given a symbolic meaning, and that is just what the biblical authors did. Throughout the Bible symbols are used to convey truth. Today, in order to understand the author's meaning, readers must translate the symbols back into the ideas the author intended. Sometimes it is difficult to grasp the meaning behind the symbol, but not often. The key to unlock the meaning lies most often in human understanding of the historical situation at the time the author wrote. Part of this understanding lies in grasping the common symbols used by other peoples of Jewish times, for modern biblical scholarship shows that Israelite literature was influenced by its contemporary pagan literature.

Numbers

One type of symbol that is most common in the Bible is numbers. Scholars have discovered that numbers had a special meaning for the Jewish mind: 7 meant totality or perfection; 6 meant imperfection; 12 meant Israel; 1000 meant immensity; 4 meant the world; 40 meant something like "sufficient for the purpose," as in Acts 1:3 where the forty-day period before Jesus' ascension meant that he spent the "time needed" to instruct his followers before his appearances ceased.

Another use the Israelites made of numbers is called *Gematria*—adding the numerical value of the letters that make up a name: e.g., a=1, b=2, d=4, etc. On one of the walls of a home in the Roman city of Pompeii (the city destroyed by a volcano in A.D. 79) can still be seen today, "I love her whose number is 545" (obviously not a telephone number!) The lover hid the name of his loved one by giving the numerical value of the letters of her name. We will see later how this *Gematria* helps us to understand the mysterious "666" image of Revelation, chapter 13.

The apocalyptic book of Daniel was written to encourage the Jewish people, who were despondent and on the verge of despair because Antiochus IV had desecrated their sacred temple with the "abomination of desolation." This was the term Jews gave to his placing a statue of the pagan god Zeus in their sanctuary. The 3½ years of persecution they underwent under this man caused them to use this number (3½ years, 1260 days, or 42 months) again and again as a symbol for any period of crisis.

Cosmic Imagery

Even more forceful as a "crisis" symbol was very picturesque cosmic imagery. It is found in biblical and nonbiblical literature alike.

For example, the Jewish work *Baba Metzia* refers to "events" associated with the excommunication of a Rabbi named Eliezer. When the news was received the author tells us: "the world was then smitten: one-third of the olive crop, one-third of the wheat, and one-third of the barley crop. Some say the dough in women's hands swelled up!"

Compare this with Revelation 6:12–17 (the sixth seal) in which John uses a similar way of speaking to dramatize the end of the persecution. J. Massyngberd Ford notes how "the order in which the universe is destroyed follows approximately the order of creation in Genesis:" creation of the earth—earthquake, sun—darkening of the sun, moon—moon turning blood red, stars—stars falling, sky—rolling up of the heavens, land—mountains and islands moved from their place, man—mankind hiding themselves.[2]

This is **not** the end of the world being described. It is simply another example of what can be termed *apocalyptic imagery:* symbolic and colorful descriptions that are "tools" (not to be taken literally) used by the biblical author to dramatize the end of the persecution and the victory that will come over Rome itself.

In a sense, it is the end of **a** world—the world of Rome and its misused power and unjust persecution. The reference is only indirectly to the end of the world as we understand the world. Additionally, these verses are to be taken only in the broad sense: at the end of time God will be clearly shown in His sovereignty and power as the forces of evil are finally silenced.

And yet, so many people today, unaware of the nature of apocalyptic imagery, have read such descriptions in the book of Revelation as prophecies of literal happenings that will someday occur. If readers can instead see these references as symbolic, their

2. J. Massyngberd Ford, *Anchor Bible Commentary on Revelation* (Garden City, NY: Doubleday, 1975), 112.

eyes and minds will be open to the many other symbols in this book, and will stop trying to guess how the symbols might refer to Russia, China, or the United States, and instead understand them as the author of Revelation wanted us to understand them.

The words of Jesus himself should be our final warning against such predictions about when the end will come: "No one knows . . . when that day or hour will come—neither the angels in heaven, nor the Son: only the Father knows." (Mark 13:32)

The Millennium

In Revelation 20:1–6 John speaks of a thousand-year period or millennium. While some see this as a precise period of time beginning in the future in preparation for or immediately following the second coming of Christ (Jehovah's Witnesses believe that it was inaugurated with the "invisible" return of Jesus to earth in 1914), Catholics follow the meaning biblical scholars find in John's own thoughts. For him, it was a symbolic—not a literal—period. *Thousand* in Scripture means *fullness, completeness.* It is the indefinite length of time that began with the life, death, and resurrection of Jesus and continues until his second coming and the final judgment of humanity. It is synonymous with Christianity, that faith-experience that stretches through history and is now swiftly approaching its two-thousandth year.

End times and *eschatology* relate to the same period. History is perceived by Christians as a series of events leading eventually to the final event, the *eschaton* in which the *Parousia* or second coming of Christ will take place "to judge the living and the dead."

The "end times" are thus a combination of "already" and "not yet." "Already" because the decisive victory over evil has already been accomplished by Christ; "not yet" because its full realization in our lives and in creation is still wanting.

With this scriptural understanding of "end times" as something already upon us today, we can better understand many images in Revelation such as "Satan chained and released," "Gog and Magog," "666 Beast," "Antichrist," and "Armageddon."

Satan Chained and Released (20:7)

What does John mean when he says that at the end of the thousand years, Satan will be released after being chained for that time? Are we to believe that God will allow evil to run rampant again after Jesus conquered evil by his death and resurrection?

Perhaps the best answer we can give is to say that evil is stubborn and persistent. Evil still remains in our midst even though Jesus overcame it (Satan chained). It's something like war: even after victory, there is still mopping up to be done. The same is true in our own lives. Although we've been converted to the Lord and really changed our former selves, we're not perfect! Many effects of the evil we and others have done still remain. And if we're not careful, evil can still pop up its ugly head, especially when our defenses are down.

Satan released is John's way of describing this reality. He is not telling his readers that at some distant period in history God will set Satan free to mislead mankind on a grand scale. Rather, he is reminding us that evil can spring up once again in our lives if we're not careful, and that despite all that Jesus has done for us, we can still finally be lost.

Gog and Magog (20:8)

John says that after one thousand years Gog and Magog will be permitted to attack the people of God. Despite Hal Lindsey's claim that Gog and Magog refer to the Soviet Union, scholarship sees them as simply "mythical summaries" of evil.

The names come from the Old Testament prophet Ezekiel, chapters 38 and 39. Genesis 10:2 lists Magog as a northern nation. They are for Ezekiel not really historical, but personifications whose features are drawn from the kings who conquered Israel, often coming from the north. John simply borrows these images. They remind us, as above, that we must never let our spiritual defenses down. For the forces of evil will again play havoc in our lives just as they may have done in the past.

The 666 Beast (13)

It would be easy to amass a lengthy list of examples illustrating anti-Catholic rhetoric in our nation today. It would be more difficult to detect whether the prejudice of those same examples stems from plain and simple bigotry or from honest ignorance. In either case, when the book of Revelation is invoked to support prejudice, this is a wrongful use of Scripture that stems from a fundamentalist manner of interpretation.

Herbert Armstrong can serve as an illustration. His World-wide Church of God published a pamphlet in 1960 entitled *Who Is The Beast?* It is still being distributed nationally free of charge. In typical literalist fashion the author, Mr. Armstrong himself, sees the Book of Revelation as strictly a future-predictor-in-detail. It takes him a while to develop his arguments but—there it is, solemnly announced on page 22: ". . . this two-horned beast, the false prophet, the man of sin and the woman that rode the beast are all one and the same thing—the Roman Catholic Church with its pope, its other bishops, its priests and deacons. . . ."

Mr. Armstrong obviously believes that misery loves company, for in a later paragraph he adds: "But this church became a mother, and daughter churches came out of her, in 'protest,' calling themselves 'Protestant.' . . . Her daughters are called 'harlots.' Together, they are called 'Babylon.' They are pagan, teaching pagan doctrines and customs, cloaked in the name of Christianity! And all nations are deceived!"

He finally ends his tract by calling for a mass exodus from these Churches with the plea: " 'Come out of her,' God says (Revelation 18:4). God help us to heed!"

Many fundamentalists seem to associate the 666 beast with Russia, especially since 1917. But they still retain an hostility to organized religion by a belief that "apostate Churches" (always including the Catholic Church) will join the mysterious Antichrist and beast in their war against the forces of the good (often associated with the American army!)

The beast and its 666 number have been in the past as much a thorn in the side for Christian unity as it is today. Critics of the Catholic Church tried to show how *Italika Ecclesia* (Greek) meaning *Italian Church,* comes to 666 when the numerical value of all the letters (*gematria*) is added together. Catholics retorted by showing the Greek *Loutherana* (Luther) and *Saxoneios* (Saxon, meaning Luther) also equals 666. Furthermore, *Maometis* (Muhammed) and *Nabonaparti* (Napoleon or Hitler) show the same result as do a hoard of additional names.[3]

3. Ford, *Anchor Revelation,* 216–217.

Obviously, many names could total 666. Hence, some "key" to the puzzle must have been provided to the people first receiving this book of Revelation. The "key," biblical scholars tell us, was the historical situation. In order to identify the person referred to by the number, one must look, as in all such apocalyptic literature, to the time contemporary with the author. Who best summarizes in the late first century the evil reflected in the image of the beast? Who was responsible for the persecution of the Christians with which the book of Revelation deals? A special person now comes to the fore: **Emperor Nero!**

In July, A.D. 64, a terrible fire broke out in Rome. It is said that Nero, seemingly a madman, started the fire. He blamed the Christians, however, and a persecution began. During this first persecution of the Church, both Peter and Paul were executed. Bishop Eusebius, the first serious Christian historian, in his *History Of The Early Church* (written in the early 400s) tells us: "It is recorded that in his (Nero's) reign Paul was beheaded in Rome itself, and that Peter likewise was crucified, and the record is confirmed . . . by a churchman named Gaius (c. A.D. 200)."

Interestingly, the same Gaius states: "I can point out the monument of the victorious apostles, if you will go as far as the Vatican (for Peter) or the Ostian Way (for Paul)."

And he was correct. Archaeologists recently unearthed the tomb of Peter directly beneath the papal altar of the present basilica of St. Peter. Over Paul's tomb stands the present-day basilica of St. Paul-Outside-the-Walls.

The name of the madman emperor Nero totals 666. Caesar Nero is written in Hebrew KSR NRWN. Giving the proper "gematria" to these Hebrew letters (K=100, S=60, R=200; N=50, R=200, W=6, N=50) produces a total of 666. In his person, Nero represents all the evil of the Roman empire (the beast). And, as will be shown very shortly, **he** (together with pagan Rome) is the infamous Antichrist!

Why does the author of Revelation speak in such hidden symbolism, so cryptically? It wasn't because he was referring to some mysterious person centuries away in history, but, according to one explanation, because of his fear of being accused of treason. If the material happened to fall into Roman hands, even sterner measures might be taken against the Church.

99

However, Scripture scholar Frank Cleary, S. J. from St. Louis University's Department of Theological Studies, in reviewing an earlier version of my material in this chapter, commented: "An increasing scholarly consensus suggests that hidden symbolism was not used to avoid persecution and detection, but that it was just part of the literary genre."

The Antichrist

The film industry has had a heyday with this image. "Damien" movies, as a case in point, were classical attempts to portray the scriptural references to Antichrist as an evil man, a special reincarnation of the devil himself, who will be coming sometime in the future, perhaps within our own period of time.

Some literature today seeks to associate the "mark of the beast" (Revelation 13:16–18) or "Antichrist" with world economic conditions. These writings explain that people will have to bear the beast's mark on their right hand or forehead, a number which will be indelible and invisible except to electronic apparatus, without which people will be unable to buy or sell. These "marks of the Antichrist" are defended according to a very literalistic and unscholarly reading of Revelation. While there may indeed be movements afoot in our fast-shrinking world to bring about better efficiency and organization, they need not be so swiftly labeled diabolical.

But the author of Revelation is not looking down through history to our twentieth century economy. Like the prophets of old, his gaze and concern are with his own time. Slaves and soldiers of that period were branded for identification, often on the hand. The author "borrows" that custom for one of his images. Likewise, with the mandated emperor worship, it was required that citizens carry a certificate showing they performed ritual sacrifice to Caesar or be subject to imprisonment and death. Revelation's author, seeing the diabolical nature of such blasphemous idolatry, exposes that evil for his Christian audience.

The name *Antichrist* is found only in John's epistles (1 John 2:18, 22; 4:3; 2 John 7). There the name is applied to the heretical movement that has been responsible for a major split in the Church. Paul speaks in 2 Thessalonians 2:3–8 of a "man of lawlessness," who seems in Paul's thought to be already in existence but somehow restrained. One interpretation applies the reference

100

to Roman emperor Caligula who, ten years earlier, tried to enthrone his own image in the Holy of Holies of Jerusalem's temple. But we need not see this "man" simply as an individual. The apocalyptic nature of the passage allows a wider application.

Although the word *Antichrist* never occurs in the book of Revelation, the beast and false prophet images all capture the same reality. Contrary to tendencies in the past and present, it is not necessary to continue to view the Antichrist as someone (something) coming in the future. Contemporary Scripture scholarship sees this mysterious figure as someone (something) already come . . . and gone! This can be seen by studying a bit of chapter 13 in Revelation.

As the reader moves through this chapter, it is clear that the beast is the antithesis of God. It is "worshipped;" the "whole world follows after" it; it is granted "authority over every race and people, language and nation." Similar language is used to describe the Lamb's (Christ's) influence in, for example, chapter 5. When chapter 13 speaks of "worshipping the beast" (Nero) the reference is to emperor worship. The Roman senate had declared five of their emperors divine after their deaths. Three of these—Claudius, Vespasian, and Titus—had the gall to even claim that honor while still living. Accordingly, they placed the word *divine* along with their images on coinage. Failure to pay godly homage to the emperor was the reason for the martyrdom of many Christians.

Both the beast and the Lamb are described "as though slain;" (chapter 13:3 for the beast and chapter 5: 6 for the Lamb). Another similarity is found in the description of the mortal wound the beast received that was, however, healed. Christ (the Lamb) was wounded unto death on the cross but was "healed" in his resurrection. Tacitus, a Roman historian, tells us that Nero was quite unpopular, especially at the end of his reign. He was repudiated by the Roman senate, proclaimed a public enemy, and finally murdered in A.D. 68 by someone who slit his throat. Fearful rumors subsequently circulated, claiming he hadn't really died and would soon regain his throne. The reference to the beast's mortal wound being healed refers, therefore, to these rumors. John doesn't give credence to the rumors but does intimate that another persecutor of the Church would follow Nero.

Two beasts are described by John, but for all practical purposes they are one and the same. As the first beast (symbolizing all that is evil in the world) is the direct opposite of God (anti-God), the sea beast is the direct opposite of the Lamb (Jesus, son of God). Hence it—the beast, which is the Roman Empire or an emperor (Nero) who embodies all the evil of the empire especially by his attack on Christians—is the infamous Antichrist!

The Antichrist is, therefore, not a special person coming in history. He (it) has already come! The Antichrist is the pagan Roman Empire that persecuted the early Christians and Caesar Nero, who so aptly summarized all the evil of that empire. The eschatological character of the Antichrist (or Paul's "man of lawlessness") is preserved because, as mentioned previously and as the *New Catholic Encyclopedia* notes: "the 'last times' commence with the first coming of Christ and extend to the Parousia.' "[4]

Armageddon (16:16)

Armageddon means "Mt. Megiddo," and refers to a famous battlefield of the Old Testament near the town of Megiddo. It was the site of battles and disasters that left a deep impression on the Jewish people, and thus became a "symbol" of catastrophe. John refers to it as "Mt." Megiddo, even though it was really a plain. He does so because he was not referring to an actual battle on the geographical Megiddo plain, but is using this sight of ancient disaster simply as a symbol for a battle that, remaining faithful to apocalyptic literature, can be seen in two ways: a battle at the **Rome** of that day or a **spiritual** battle.

First: a battle at **Rome**. John envisions, as a punishment for Rome's unfaithfulness and persecution of Christians, that this city-empire will be invaded by the enemies of Rome, especially the nearby Parthians. The old legend of Nero's return again to the throne located him in Parthia, plotting to use the Parthian army to secure his throne at Rome once again. John, of course, doesn't believe Nero actually does live again, but he believes Nero's spirit is pervading the enemies of Rome.

English Scripture scholar G. B. Caird says it so well:

> *It must now be apparent how impossible it is to maintain that, when John set out to give warning about "what is bound to happen soon" (1:1), he included in these*

4. *New Catholic Encyclopedia,* vol. 1 (New York: McGraw-Hill, 1967), 618.

immediate expectations the end of the world. The ut-
most limit of his prophetic vision was the end of Rome's
world which he believed to be inherent in her forth-
coming persecution of the Church. In her attack on the
Church, Rome would let loose into the world powers
which would compass her own downfall.[5]

Second: a **spiritual** battle. The symbol of Armageddon can be
simply seen as a mythical image of the ever-recurring theme running through Revelation of good battling evil during the length
of history but eventually registering a decisive victory. It occurs
in my and your lives most specifically at the time of our deaths
when we summarize for all eternity the victories we won over sin
in our daily life struggles. Death is, in a sense, our individual Ar-
mageddons; but as long as the history of humankind continues,
the final resolution of the conflict will still be elusive. Someday,
at a time that God alone knows, good will finally conquer evil. But
this will be a spiritual victory won through a spiritual struggle—
not a physical battle or war. Our battle, as Paul tells us, is "not
against human forces but against the principalities and powers"
(Ephesians 6:12). To state, as Hal Lindsey does in *Countdown To
Armageddon,* that the symbol of Armageddon is referring to
some major physical war of our day or some day in our future
is a complete misunderstanding of the book of Revelation and
the nature of apocalyptic literature. It is a classic example of
s t r e t c h i n g the sacred text to say something it really doesn't
say!

The unbridled arms race could well indeed usher in the destruction of our planet. But this is not something the book of Revelation addresses. When we misapply Scripture's "prophecies" to
our day, there is a terrible danger that we may create a scenario
reflecting our vision. A belief that Armageddon is an impending
physical battle between "good" and "evil" nations can easily cause
nations to continue stockpiling nuclear weapons for the confron-
tation. Such misguided religious beliefs could even initiate a nuclear conflagration, for we are more likely to fire nuclear weapons
if we are convinced it is now the predicted time for their use!

5. G. B. Caird, *The Revelation of St. John the Divine* (London: Adam and
Charles Black, 1966), 209.

Can it be said too many times? The biblical Armageddon of Revelation is **not** a prediction of a nuclear catastrophe. Religious enthusiasts must stop spreading that illusion lest they bear the responsibility for building a climate for World War III!

The Message Today

The message of Revelation responds to a critical problem in our own time. By now every Catholic is surely aware of the great number of Catholics who have "dropped out" of Church life. Some of our young people are attracted to cults that belittle beliefs revered from the most ancient times: the Trinity, the divinity of Jesus, Jesus as *the* revelation of God, the need for (even the value of) the Church. Various types of gurus sap the time, talents, and financial earnings of youths misled by their empty promises—gurus who become a substitute for Jesus.

Revelation reminds us that such forms of idolatry are not unique to history. We are merely experiencing twentieth century expressions of what plagued the early Church. Many of our people are falling under the illusory spell of these charlatans and movements for various reasons, not the least of which is a failure to beware of their temptations.

The churches of Pergamum and Thyatira (Revelation 2) were plagued by a group termed *Nicolaitans,* who were influencing Christians into a compromise with the world. Religion was merely spiritual, they argued, and a follower of Christ could live pretty much as the pagans around him as long as he "spiritually" (in mind and spirit) adhered to Christ. Things of the flesh or body were of little account because only the spirit is worthy of God. This being the case, it mattered little if Christians shared in, for example, emperor worship, just as long as they followed Jesus "in spirit."

The church at Pergamum was thus reflecting, in its acquiescence to Nicolaitan beliefs, a tendency of the Church down through history. That tendency was and is not only to live **in** the world but to become part **of** it.[6] Revelation's author tells them to stop straddling the fence: choose between Christ and Caesar!

6. Caird, *John the Divine,* 37–45.

In the mid-second century, an anonymous "Letter to Diognetus" was written describing Christians and their relationship to the world around them. It spells out what John was saying:

> *Christians . . . live in their own country as though they were only passing through. . . . Any country can be their homeland, but for them their homeland, wherever it may be, is a foreign country. . . . They live in the flesh, but they are not governed by the desires of the flesh. They pass their days upon earth, but they are citizens of heaven. . . . The Christian is to the world what the soul is to the body. As the soul is present in every part of the body, while remaining distinct from it, so Christians are found in all the cities of the world, but cannot be identified with the world.*

Many Christians today miss that distinction. They try to live too much like the world and are, as a result, compromising their Christianity, losing the flavor of their "first love" for Christ. Reading John's warning to the early churches of Pergamum and Thyatira should inspire modern readers to return to the fervor of their original dedication to Jesus at the time of their baptisms. Metanoia, ongoing conversion, is the basic theme running through all dimensions of the Christian life.

Although history marches on, those who live through successive stages of history are really not vastly different from those living in those early centuries. As in John's time, evil today is concealed in very attractive trappings. John used offensive symbols (beasts, whore, Babylon) to describe the evil he perceived, because that evil came on so attractively. He had to unmask it, especially the attractiveness of pagan Rome, for what it really was.

That problem is still with us today. We never directly choose something we see as evil. We choose an evil because, at least for the moment, it seems attractive and good. We thus become ensnared in wrongdoing.

Take two examples—first, our tendency to create and worship false gods. This appears today in the form of cults such as the Peoples' Temple under apparently sick and mad Jim Jones, a community so attractive to so many, but laden with insidious forces of leader worship and blind suicidal obedience. The attractions for its adherents were as subtle as those experienced by early Christians for pagan Rome. False gods can take other attractive forms: anyone or anything in one's life that takes the place of God— money, power, pleasure.

A second example is John's description of Rome as the great whore, drunk in her fornications. Rome is the great whore because she seduced nations to false worship.

The Old Testament saw the relationship between the people and God as a marriage bond. Sin, the breaking of that relationship, was described therefore as "unfaithfulness," "adultery," or "fornication." But John surely had also in mind the literal sexual attractions of Rome, for historians describe Rome's downfall as being caused to a good extent by its moral depravity.

Today's sexual revolution is no less insidious. It is attractive to many because it seems "so nice." Movies and television, in particular, portray casual sexual affairs as simply a part of life, contributing to happiness, personal joy, and fulfillment. It is illusory. Revelation warns us to beware the apparent attraction and remember the evil that is involved, an evil that can be seen in the results of casual, uncommitted sex: psychological problems, unhappiness, abortion, division between people, marital breakdowns.

But Revelation is not only a warning against evil. It is also (and this is its primary message) a promise of hope. God is on our side. With His help and following His guidance, we can and will conquer that and every evil.

Review and Discussion

1. What is the meaning of *apocalyptic* literature?

2. How is apocalyptic literature *prophetic?*

3. Who is the great enemy of God in Revelation? How do we know?

4. Explain the millennium.

5. How should we understand Satan's *chaining?*

6. Who is the 666 beast? Why?

7. Who is the Antichrist? Why?

8. Discuss the meaning of Armageddon, and give examples of how it is being misunderstood today.

9. What does Revelation say to you?

Appendix

There are several additional points raised by fundamentalist beliefs that could not comfortably be included in preceding chapters but still merit special attention.

The Denial of Tradition

What we learn from Scripture . . . depends very much on how we have been taught to read and interpret Scripture. It also depends on the questions and expectations we have been taught to bring to the study of Scripture.[1]

Fundamentalists hold that there is no need for outside help in understanding what the Bible says or means. God alone aids them in their reading. Nor is there any need for resources other than Scripture to understand the things of God. They reject the necessity for a Church's official interpretation of Scripture as well as the value of insights and guidance from Tradition.

Catholics have a different approach. Although we also believe that God inspires and directs our lives as we read and reflect on His Word, we see a real need for scholarly insights and Church guidance. Together they comprise the ongoing Tradition of the Church.

1. Monika K. Hellwig, *Understanding Catholicism* (Ramsey, NJ: Paulist Press, 1981), 3.

Vatican II's *Dogmatic Constitution on Divine Revelation* shows how Catholics view the connection between Scripture and Tradition (emphasis added):

> *Hence, there exists a close connection and communication between sacred tradition and Sacred Scripture. For both of them, flowing from the same divine wellspring, in a certain way merge into a unity and tend toward the same end. . . .* **Consequently it is not from Sacred Scripture alone that the Church draws her certainty about everything which has been revealed.** *Therefore both sacred tradition and Sacred Scripture are to be accepted and venerated with the same sense of loyalty and reverence.*[2]

> **Sacred tradition and Sacred Scripture form one sacred deposit of the word of God, committed to the Church.**[3]

In section 8 the Constitution explains this Tradition more clearly. It states how **the apostolic preaching is expressed in a special way in the inspired books of the Bible,** how **this Tradition from the apostles**

> *develops in the Church with the help of the Holy Spirit. For there is a growth in the understanding of the realities and the words which have been handed down.*

This growth takes place

> *through the contemplation and study made by believers, who treasure these things in their hearts (see Luke 2:19, 51), through a penetrating understanding of the spiritual realities which they experience, and through the preaching of those who have received through episcopal succession the sure gift of truth. For as the centuries succeed one another, the Church constantly moves forward toward the fullness of divine truth until the words of God reach their complete fulfillment in her.*[4]

2. Abbott, *Documents Vatican II,* "Revelation," section 9, page 117.
3. Abbott, *Documents Vatican II,* "Revelation," section 10, page 117.
4. Abbott, *Documents Vatican II,* "Revelation," section 8, page 116.

At the end of section 10, the Constitution summarizes:

> *It is clear, therefore, that sacred tradition, Sacred Scripture and the teaching authority of the Church, in accord with God's most wise design, are so linked and joined together that one cannot stand without the others, and that all together and each in its own way under the action of the one Holy Spirit contribute effectively to the salvation of souls.*[5]

Tradition referred to here is not the same thing as traditions. The former reflects the important elements of Christian faith, its doctrines that guide us in our understanding of God and His plan for us. On the other hand, traditions are merely surface issues open to easy change or alteration. Examples of traditions would be kneeling or standing in church, the color of Mass vestments, the size of communion hosts, the wearing of head-coverings in church by women and other such customs that have no important connection with the essentials of religion.

Tradition spelled with a capital "T" grows from many sources. Official professions of faith such as our Apostles' Creed and the Mass's Niceno-Constantinopolitan Creed crystallized early Christian doctrines. The Councils of Nicea (325), Constantinople (381), Ephesus (431) and Chalcedon (451) explained who Jesus was and what he meant for us. Writings of the Fathers of the Church or groups of bishops; teachings of the Popes; even Christian art (as in stained glass windows), music, drama, sermons—all contributed (and contribute today) to the formation of Church teaching and belief.

The Catholic understanding of revelation is indeed a far cry from the limited approach of fundamentalists. They not only limit themselves to the Bible, but usually to a very restricted method of reading the Bible, a method that gives infallible credence to an English translation (King James) that itself suffers from deficiencies of old English and from poor manuscripts used in translation. Further limitations occur because of a failure to accept the guidance of scholarship or teaching authority, a denial of literary forms, a refusal to admit any form of historical, scientific, or time-conditioned religious errors.

---

5. Abbott, *Documents Vatican II*, "Revelation," section 10, page 118.

The richness of the Catholic approach is in stark contrast. For us, the Bible is a living, vibrant communication of the Word of God within the context of a believing community. Our belief is in a God who continues an ongoing dialogue of self-communication that is realized through the Church's prayerful reflection on His once-spoken but never ended scriptural revelation.

"Are You Saved, Brother?"

Catholics usually have a hard time responding to the question from fundamentalist neighbors: "Are you saved?" We find it hard to answer because we find it hard to understand.

If the questioner elaborates by asking: "Do you accept Jesus Christ as your personal savior?", we feel more at ease. "Of course," we reply. But we're still a little edgy in the suspicion that the question seems to avoid the critical role of community. We come to know Jesus in and through the Church and serve him in our fellow human beings. A strong "me-Jesus" spirituality too easily ignores the horizontal dimension of Christianity, the need for a loving relationship with others if we plan to have heaven as our eternal mailing address.

Our answer therefore to the question "Are you saved?" must usually be: **yes** and **no**. **Yes**, because we do believe that we are indeed saved in and by Jesus Christ, but **no** in the sense that salvation is something that ultimately depends on a free gift of God, a gift we can never be absolutely certain is ours until the moment of our deaths.

In other words, we see a large distinction between the statement "I am saved by Jesus" and the statement, "I personally will be saved in the next life," because that salvation will be effective for me only if I truly live my Catholic Christian faith. By his life, death, and resurrection, Jesus saved all peoples, but are all therefore going to automatically gain heaven?

The Catholic Church views salvation as a pure and free gift of God. God gives it freely to His children, and absolutely nothing that we do, no matter how good a life we live, can ever allow us to put ourselves in a position of saying: "Now, God, you **owe** me salvation!"

Scripture clearly teaches, as in 1 Corinthians 9:27 ("What I do is discipline my own body and master it, for fear that after having preached to others I myself should be rejected"), that we can never in this life be absolutely certain of our eternal salvation. But by adhering to Jesus Christ in a personal love relationship, following his commandments and teachings especially by loving and serving others, and listening to the guidance he gives us through his Church, we can have a genuine sense of comfort in the realization that God rewards those who love and serve Him.

The Catholic approach to salvation combines texts such as Galatians 2:16 (". . . knowing that a man is not justified by legal observance but by faith in Jesus Christ") and James 2:24, 26 ("You must perceive that a person is justified by his works and not by faith alone. . . . Be assured, then, that faith without works is as dead as a body without breath"). Vatican II sounded the same warning for Church members by teaching that "he is not saved, however, who, though he is part of the body of the Church, does not persevere in charity. He remains indeed in the bosom of the Church, but, as it were, only in a 'bodily' manner and not 'in his heart.' "[6]

Catholic hesitation in responding to the question "Are you saved?" is due to the fact that it seems to make salvation a one-time event in a person's life. Salvation for us is a long-term "process" that begins with our baptism and continues through our faithfulness to God in everyday living. In 1 Peter 3:21 we read: "You are now saved by a baptismal bath. . . ." But other Scripture texts make it clear that our eternally secure union with God will not be a final reality unless a good and virtuous life follows that baptism.

A final point should be made here. Unlike the belief of many fundamentalists, Catholics stress that God's salvation can come to people who are not explicit Christians. We believe that Jesus is the way for all, that salvation is always in him ("No one comes to the Father but through me" John 14:6), but that many travel that way unknowingly. Vatican II summarizes the Church's teaching:

> *Those also can attain to everlasting salvation who through no fault of their own do not know the gospel of Christ or his Church, yet sincerely seek God and, moved by grace, strive by their deeds to do his will as it is known*

6. Abbott, *Documents Vatican II,* "Church," section 14, page 33.

113

to them through the dictates of conscience. Nor does divine Providence deny the help necessary for salvation to those who, without blame on their part, have not yet arrived at an explicit knowledge of God, but who strive to live a good life, thanks to his grace.[7]

These people admittedly have a tougher road to travel, but God's love enfolds everyone and He will offer to all the grace to be saved.

Will There Be a Rapture?

Before coming to West Virginia in 1973, I had never heard the term *rapture* in the context in which it is used in these mountains. And when I did hear it for the first time, I had no clear idea what it meant. The English word *rapture* means simply an ecstatic joy or delight. What did people mean who spoke of a rapture at the end time? I later discovered that it is a belief of "born-again"[8] Christian fundamentalists that there will be a generation of people who will not see death. They will experience instead a "rapture," a being taken up alive with Jesus into the clouds.

The belief comes especially from 1 Thessalonians 4:16–17:

> . . . *those who have died in Christ will rise first. Then we the living, the survivors, will be caught up with them in the clouds to meet the Lord in the air.*

The primary question, when interpreting any text of Scripture, is not what I believe it means, but: What did the author who wrote it mean? To discover that, we have to examine more than just the words of the text itself but, as has already been discussed, the entire literary background to the text. Scholars can help us bring to our Scripture reading a much broader and deeper understanding by enlightening us about that background, about the literary form used by the author.

The text in question (1 Thessalonians 4:16–17) is a very symbolic passage. Like other apocalyptic literature (Revelation is the classic example), the author is merely using images to convey

---

7. Abbott, *Documents Vatican II,* "Church," section 16, page 35.
8. *Born-again* simply means the experience of new life that results from God's love pouring into one's soul. Fundamentalist Christians use it to refer to a religious experience (usually highly emotional) that thereby indicates a person is "saved."

more basic points. Essentially he is teaching, under God's inspiration, that those who have died before the second coming of Christ at the end of time will share in his glorious resurrection. Being "caught up in the clouds" reflects the simplistic cosmology of the time. As Jesus comes down from clouds, believers go up into clouds to meet him halfway.

Furthermore, Paul is stressing that we just do not know when Christ will make his appearance: "The day of the Lord is coming like a thief in the night" (1 Thessalonians 5:2). Fundamentalists, in seeing our late twentieth century as the forewarned "end of time," expect the second coming of Christ very soon.

In 1 Thessalonians, Paul was reflecting a similar belief of the early Church that Jesus' second coming was right around the corner. Paul himself shared that belief: "We the living will be caught up." In 2 Thessalonians, the Church and Paul faced the reality of an indefinite delay in the second coming:

> *On the question of the coming of Our Lord Jesus Christ and our being gathered to him, we beg you, brothers, not to be so easily agitated or terrified . . . into believing that the day of the Lord is here. (2 Thessalonians 2:1–2)*

That Christ will come again "in glory to judge the living and the dead" is a firm Christian belief with a solid scriptural base. That some will experience a "rapture" into the clouds is a mistaken interpretation, a too-literalistic reading of a very symbolic scriptural text of Paul. "Then we the living will be caught up with them (risen dead) in the clouds" merely reflects Paul's expectation to be alive when Christ would soon come, and has no reference to any privileged group of the future suddenly "disappearing" while at work at the end time. Besides being a misinterpretation of Scripture, this belief has the danger of encouraging believers to pridefully consider themselves a special elite that looks down on everyone not to be so caught up as "those sinners!"

Afterword

I sincerely hope the preceding chapters haven't come across too harshly. Fundamentalists, despite their differences, remain our brothers and sisters in Christ. But the conflicts they stir by their resolute adherence to a literalistic interpretation of Scripture—including hostility towards biblical scholarship and the facility with which many of them place all mainline churches, especially the Catholic Church, within the ranks of the forces of evil—remind us of how through the ages Christianity's worst enemy has been its own divided membership.

Psalm 55:13–15 gives expression to the sorrow, the disappointment we feel in our family separateness:

> *If an enemy had reviled me,*
>   *I could have borne it;*
> *If he who hates me had vaunted himself against me,*
>   *I might have hidden from him.*
> *But you, my other self,*
>   *my companion and my bosom friend!*
> *You, whose comradeship I enjoyed,*
>   *at whose side I walked in procession in the house of*
>   *God!*

Disagreements have rocked and split the followers of Christ since the earliest days of the Church. But the wide proliferation of enemies of Christ today is demanding more than ever before that Christians work with a revolutionary fervor to establish unity in order to meet the onslaught. Worldwide terrorism, joined with anti-God forces are our enemies; we should not be each other's enemies.

Catholics need their fundamentalist neighbors, and they need us. Catholics rejoice in how those who adhere to fundamentalism are so strongly opposed to abortion on demand, the pornography industry, and a secular humanism that excludes the place of God and the supernatural.

When so many today seem all too ready to compromise traditional Christian moral tenets, fundamentalism's dogged adherence to those same tenets is a needed shot in the arm. Even if we are not able to agree on all issues, our unity, our corporate witness, would offer a much needed alternative to the lack of faith and the resultant increasing moral depravity running through the American way of life.

The key to that unity is a change—or at least an openness on the part of fundamentalists—to a method of biblical interpretation other than fundamentalist-literalistic. There is no biblical justification for including the Catholic Church, the Pope, bishops, priests, religious, or laity in the camp of satanic influence. Catholics writhe in just anger when fundamentalists make that connection with their application of literalistic tools to the book of Revelation.[1] How can any form of genuine peace exist between us as long as such prejudice continues?

What fundamentalists most need is an education into the principles of biblical interpretation, the development of a frame of mind, a way of approaching the Bible stories, events, and people that incorporates an understanding of the literary forms used by the authors of Scripture. The Bible must be seen as a theology book, not a history or science book. Religious teaching is the all-important element. And the message of God's Word can never be divorced from the cultural setting, the background in which it was written.

It's a terrible shame that the years of work scholars have done on Scripture and the insights that have resulted from that labor of

---

1. They correctly observe that the enemy in the book of Revelation is Rome. But since they view this final Bible book as a future-predictor in detail, thus ignoring its apocalyptic form, they associate the Rome of today (instead of 2000-year-ago pagan Rome) with that enemy. And what is found in Rome today? The Vatican!

love are denied to vast groups of Christians because of the limitations they place on themselves by approaching the Bible literalistically. Proper scriptural education is sorely needed among the many followers of Christ.

If we don't take serious steps to counteract literalism in the reading of Scripture, we will continue to see evangelization falter and ecumenism suffer. (How can any form of rapprochement come about if the Catholic Church is considered by so many fundamentalists as God's enemy?) The poorly educated will be increasingly confirmed in their lack of understanding (Catholics included, to the point of even being lured into fundamentalist Churches)—those same individuals who are supposed to occupy a special place in the Church's concern, love, and educational care!

Index

Roman Empire, 92, 99, 102
Russia, 98

S
Salt, Lot's wife pillar of, 20 (footnote)
Sacred prostitution, 77
Satan, 81–82
    chained and released, 97
Saul, death of, 62–63
"Saved," 112–114
Scholarship,
    Church approval of, 9–10, 11,
       13–16, 91ff
    Church resistance to, 8–11
    fundamentalists and, 54
    need for, 1–5
Sciatic muscle, 21
Science,
    Genesis and, 73ff
    Pontifical Academy of, 60–61
    true, 75–76
Scripture,
    alone, 9
    authorship of, 15–16, 61, 71
    Church rulings on meanings of, 11
    importance of, 4, 5, 9
    meanings of, 11–12
    truths, 16 (cf. Inerrancy)
Second coming of Christ, 114–115
Sense,
    fuller, 46ff
    literal, 11–12
    typical, 47ff
Serpent,
    bronze, 48
    in garden, 81–82
Sexual promiscuity and Susanna, 25
Sexuality, part of creation, 74
Sheol, 35
Sin, spread of, 83–84
Snake handling, 56

Solar system, 73
Sons of god, daughters of men, 84
Sun, standing still, 25ff
Susanna, 25
Symbolic action, 32
Symbolism, 93–94

T
Temple, clearing of: when?, 63
Terah, 88–89
Tetragrammaton (YHWH), 77
Texts, problem, 62ff
Textual criticism, 39ff
Theory in science, 76
"Till" she brought forth, 53
"Time-conditioned" religious beliefs,
    15–16
Tobit, 23–24
Tradition, 53
    Catholic Church and, 109–111
    fundamentalism's denial of, 109
Translations of Bible, 39
Truth of Scripture, 16, 49, 65
    and symbolism, 93–94
Typical sense of Scripture, 47ff

U–V–W
Virgin, Isaiah 7:14, 47
Virginity of Mary, 53
Wisdom literature, 34ff
    meaning of, 34–35
Words of Jesus,
    authenticity of, 41ff
    meaning lost in translation, 43–44

X–Y–Z
Yahwist, 71ff, 77–79, 85
YHWH (Tetragrammaton), 77
    (footnote)
Ziggurat, 88

Selected Readings

The following books are also available from the Religious Education Division of the Wm. C. Brown Company Publishers:

Beginners' Guide to Bible Sharing

Beginner's Guide to Bible Sharing is designed to aid persons who do not have formal theological or scriptural training.

It provides a basic approach to using the Bible in establishing a firm foundation for personal spiritual growth.

The two books form a program of group sessions that involve discussion, sharing, prayer, and reflection.

The four objectives of each session are to discover knowledge, understanding, application, and evaluation.

Volume I gives introductory information and suggestions for setting up the program, how to use the books and facilitate the sessions, 30 session outlines for greater themes of the Bible and 30 session outlines covering the Acts of the Apostles.

Volume II provides 30 session outlines covering a study of the Gospel According to Luke and 30 session outlines concentrating on Letters to the Romans.

Beginners' Guide to Bible Sharing is written by John Burke, O.P.

Volume I, (#2014)

Volume II, (#2015)

Understanding the Bible

Written by Ronald J. Wilkins.

The objective of this introductory source book is to help students explore the Bible as a work of literature and, more importantly, as God's revelation to people.

Through special research projects contained in the text, students not only develop a working knowledge of the Bible, but also a clearer understanding of what the Bible is, what it says, and what it means.

Numerous maps and charts pinpoint events, locations, and scriptural references. A word list, index, and supplemental readings are some of the study helps included.

SUPPLEMENTS *Understanding the Bible* is available in both school and parish editions. *Bible Probes* is a spirit master booklet containing 14 in-class activities, 5 overhead transparencies, and a course evaluation form. It may be used with both editions.

These materials are also valuable for adult groups who are beginning Bible study.

School Edition, (#1786)

Teacher Edition, (#1787)

Parish Edition, (#1659)

Teacher Manual, (#1665)

Bible Probes, (#1670)

Reading the New Testament

Written by Ronald J. Wilkins.

A widely-used source book, *Reading the New Testament* guides high school students or adults in a study of not only the content and development of the New Testament, but also the message of the Gospels and the revelation of Jesus.

Students learn the historical background of the New Testament and how to use the New Testament as their primary source. Through reflection, they are helped to find the meaning of Jesus in their own lives.

SUPPLEMENTS *Reading the New Testament* is available in both a parish and school edition. *Insights* is a spirit master booklet containing 16 in-class activities and 4 transparencies that is available for use with both editions.

School Edition, (#1810)

Teacher Manual, (#1811)

Parish Edition, (#1673)

Teacher Manual, (#1680)

Spirit Masters, (#1674)

The Jesus Book

Written by Ronald J. Wilkins.

Subtitled "What the New Testament Tells Us about Jesus," this high school text is designed to help students understand why Jesus is the most important person who ever lived.

The book also discusses why Christians believe that Jesus is the Son of God and what this belief means in the students' lives and in the lives of people around them.

Chapter summaries; questions for discussion, research, and review; words-to-know; and things-to-remember are some of the study helps included in this text.

SUPPLEMENTS *The Jesus Book* is available in both a parish and school edition. *Lord and Savior, Friend and Brother* is a spirit master booklet containing 15 in-class activities that may be used with both editions.

School Edition, (#1917)

Teacher Manual, (#1927)

Parish Edition, (#1695)

Teacher Manual, (#1714)

Spirit Masters, (#1692)

Journeying with Christ

Journeying with Christ is a series of books, each on a different topic, which offers adults opportunities to reflect on the Scripture, the teachings of Christ and the Church, and stories of faith. Through this reflection, readers can come to a deeper understanding and appreciation of the Christian life.

Each book in *Journeying with Christ* follows the same basic format and has the following features:

STORIES which lead more readily to personal reflection. INFORMATION in nontechnical language. SCRIPTURE that links your story with the story of God. PERSONAL REFLECTION aided by short questions. PERSONAL DECISIONS for living the Christian life. DISCUSSION for sharing insights.

Journeying with Christ is written by **Rev. William A. Anderson**. The books may be used alone or in groups. The books in the series are:

Journeying through the RCIA

A journey to help adults understand what the RCIA can mean to both the parish community and to individuals within the community. (#1941)

Journeying toward Baptism

A journey of preparing for Baptism by reflecting on the unique and personal experience of the birth, the family, the child, the religious community, and the sacrament itself. (#2002)

Journeying toward Marriage

A journey reflecting on the couple's relationship and the sacrament of marriage as a lifetime commitment. (#2059)

In His Light

This readable and concise resource presents the basics of Catholic faith along with current thoughts and trends developing within the Church. Each chapter is preceded by an allegory (which is excellent for meditations) and the book concludes with an index of Catholic prayers and practices. Written by **Rev. William A. Anderson**. (#2111)

Journeying in His Light

This formation guide presents 35 topics and session outlines. Using chapters from *In His Light* as background, sessions begin with a series of scripture references and include questions for discussion and reflection. Space is provided for composing personal thoughts and prayers. Each session concludes with a simple prayer. Written by **Rev. William A. Anderson**. (#1858)

RCIA: Foundations of Christian Initiation

Providing a general introduction to Christian Initiation as well as guidelines and starters for its implementation is the focus of this reference. The book covers the different stages of initiation, its history, and the special issues regarding initiation. Commissioned by the Archdiocese of Dubuque, Office of Religious Education. (#1781)

RCIA: A Practical Approach to Christian Initiation

To help restore the catechumenate structure, this book offers a complete guide for implementing the Rite of Christian Initiation. It provides program sessions, worksheets, and outlines for the rites, and guidelines for facilitating the program. Written by a five-member ministry team. (#1759)

Evangelization, the Catechumenate, and Its Ministries

As an integral part of the Church's mission, evangelization—both as a vision and an involvement—is the topic of this book. Designed to go beyond the renewal ritual of the catechumenate, the book discusses evangelization in relation to a variety of areas such as different ministries and sacraments. Written by Lise M. Holash. (#1868)

Shared Faith is for the single, the married, the divorced, the widowed, and the elderly. It provides the resources and experiential techniques that address adults as adults. Written by Mary Jo Tully, each book in the *Shared Faith* series includes a collection of resource readings for the participants. Following each reading are two or three questions that call for the reader's reflection on how the reading relates to his or her personal life.

Included in each *Shared Faith* book is a guide for the group facilitator. It provides a four-step session outline consisting of an activity focusing on some dimension of the topic, exploring, discussing, and reflecting on the topic; scriptural reading, and prayer. These session outlines include music suggestions and additional discussion starters.

The four books of the *Shared Faith* series are:

Blessed Be

Nine sessions in which the adults are urged to discuss the Beatitudes in light of their own experience and belief.

Readings include: Blessed Poverty, Blessed the Gentle, Happy the Mourner, The Hunger Within, Beyond the Law, and Blessed the Pure in Heart. (#1822)

Church: A Faith-Filled People

Ten sessions focusing on the Church as a community where adults share caring, loving, and belonging through God and each other.

Readings include: We Are a Community, Love Does Such Things for Us, With Thanks to the Father, Our Forgiving God, and One in the Spirit. (#1823)

Psalms: Faith Songs for the Faith-Filled

Eight sessions for adults to increase their appreciation of the Psalms and the enrichment they bring to prayer.

Readings include: One with the Father, We Believe, Out of Nothing, Sing a Song of Freedom, and Ever Faithful. (#1824)

No Other God: A Spirituality of the Ten Commandments

Newest in the *Shared Faith* series, contains eight resource readings and sessions for reflection upon and study of the Commandments.

Readings include: I Am Lord, My Name Is Holy, A Day in Honor of Yahweh, And the Two Shall Be As One, and Choose Life. (#1942)

Imagine That!

This creative resource discusses imagination, emotions, and phantasies as contributors to awareness, decision making, and motivation. Also covered is the use of phantasies in spiritual direction.

Imagine That! also contains 15 presentations that engage participants in a phantasy and then ask for reflection, meaning, and insight resulting from it. The phantasies can be used by an individual or a group. The phantasies are divided into three sections: Exploring Yourself, Exploring Your Relationship, and Exploring the Terrain Around You.

Also available is a 60-minute video cassette which demonstrates and discusses using phantasies. Following that are two phantasies complete with visual reflection/prayer meditation. The video is presented by the program's author, Marlene Halpin, Dominican.

    #1812 Book

        Video Cassette

   1838 ¾" U-Matic

   1839 ½" VHS

   1840 ½" Beta I

   1841 ½" Beta II/III

Christian Spirituality for the Eighties

Just released, this new resource presents four separate papers dealing with different facets and approaches of spiritual development. Authors are Claire Lowery (who is also the editor), Howard Grey, S.J., Rosemary Haughton, and Peggy Way. (#1940)

Year of the Lord, Reflections on the Sunday Readings

Whether for individual reflection or informal group enrichment, these books are for Catholics interested in personal reflection on the three Sunday Scripture readings. For each Sunday and major feast of the liturgical year, there is a citation of the readings, summary statements establishing the theme for each, a reflection on a general theme suggested by all the readings, and a prayer response. Written by Rev. Alfred McBride, O.Praem. Cycle A (#1847), Cycle B (#1848), Cycle C (#1849)

For further information, contact:

WM. C. BROWN COMPANY PUBLISHERS
Religious Education Division
P.O. Box 539; 2460 Kerper Blvd.
Dubuque, IA 52001
(319) 589–2833